PROTEST [3]

RED

BLACK

BROWN

EXPERIENCE IN AMERICA

by

James Mencarelli and Steve Severin

William B. Eerdmans Publishing Company

Copyright © 1975 by Wm. B. Eerdmans Publishing Company
Grand Rapids, Michigan
All rights reserved
Printed in the United States of America

Library of Congress Cataloging in Publication Data

Mencarelli, James R   1942–

  Protest[3] Red, Black, Brown experience in America.

    Bibliography: p. 197.
    1. Negroes. 2. Mexican Americans. 3. Indians of
North America. I. Severin, Steve, 1946–   joint
author. II. Title.
E184.A1M39   301.45'1'0973   74-31365
ISBN 0-8028-1598-7

Contents

Foreword

ON AN ISLAND CALLED "LIBERTY" in the harbor of New York City is a statue famous the world over for what it claims to symbolize about America. On a tablet in the pedestal of that statue is a poem entitled "The New Colossus," which, speaking of America as "the Mother of Exiles," says in part:

> *Give me your tired, your poor,*
> *Your huddled masses yearning to breathe free,*
> *The wretched refuse of your teeming shore.*
> *Send these, the homeless, tempest-tossed to me:*
> *I lift my lamp beside the golden door.*

And so they came, these "exiles." They came by the thousands. By the tens of thousands. By the millions. They came from Ireland. They came from France. They came from Germany, Latvia, Estonia, Hungary, Slovakia, Poland, Spain, Italy, Sweden, Denmark, Wales, Sicily, Austria, Greece, and Russia. They were deposited on the shores of Manhattan Island, eventually to disperse themselves across this vast continent where there was a nation in the making—*America*. A new civilization was being born—*American*. These "huddled masses," this "wretched refuse," these "tempest-tossed," these "exiles" were in due time to become partners in a great enterprise, participants in an experiment based on a self-evident truth—that all men are created equal and are endowed by their Creator with certain unalienable rights.

Those who came, came in pursuit of a more complete

realization of those rights than was possible in the lands they left behind. They came looking for a better life than they had known in the Old Country. Wider freedoms. Better opportunities. They were looking for escape. Escape from fear. Escape from want. Escape from persecution: religious persecution; economic persecution; political persecution; racial persecution. They came looking to live in the light rather than in the shadows. They were looking for a chance to uncover their own candles and lift them up; to make their own contributions in terms of those grand, new perspectives this land would offer them. Wretched refuse? History would tell.

Often enough these were people full of tragedy; but always they were people full of hope and full of dreams. They were people full of promise, and their promise was in part the promise of America. These were the parents—once removed, twice removed, perhaps three times removed—of that "silent majority" (and that "vocal minority") who helped make America what it was, and what it is. These were America's "ethnics"—people with names that were hard to spell and harder to pronounce. So a boisterous, riotous America, with her manners still incipient and her sensibilities dulled perhaps by the exigencies of nation-building, gave these ethnics simple, uncomplicated names that every *American* could pronounce. The proper associations and assignments for the names were of course automatic. They were called "Dagoes," "Micks," "Hunkies," "Kikes," "Ginks," "Pollacks," "Paddys," and the like. Life was not always easy for these Ethnics who had come looking for America's golden door. But they stayed on. They worked hard. They became Americans, and eventually a lot of other Americans learned to say their names. It came to pass— selectively at first, and then more generally—that the rest of America forgot that they were "Kikes" and "Pollacks," "Dagoes" and "Hunkies." They were *Americans,* and as such they prospered and found their respective niches in the American scheme of things.

When the Ethnics arrived, the Anglo-Saxons were already here, of course. They set the norms, defined the roles, and marked off the parameters of participation. (After all, it was *their* experiment!) Coincidentally, the Indians were already here. But they had been effectively dispossessed and pacified.

Indeed, by the flood-tide of Ethnic immigration the Indians had been so devastated and subdued as to make their subsequent assignment to the romantic and honorific role of "Noble Savage" a bitterly ironical promotion. Having practically eliminated the Indian from the land, a generous and forgiving America was more than willing to give him a secure place in the *romance* of America. So the likeness of the Red Man was stamped on the low denominations of the nation's coinage; and the nation's Boy Scouts studied the Indian lore and distinguished their troops with tribal names and artifacts and symbols. But the country's real estimate of the Indian was more often depicted in the romanticization of the American cowboy, the American cavalry, and "the winning of the West," an episode in which the only good Indians were those who were good and dead.

When the Ethnics got to America the Blacks were already here too, in large numbers. They had been around awhile—the first ones came with Columbus—but their part in the experiment at Jamestown and during the better part of two and a half centuries following was that of slaves. Not infrequently, however, they rejected their assigned roles and made common cause with the Indians. This practice was politically (and economically) embarrassing to a government committed to Black slavery and Red extermination, so a war was fought and the Indians remaining in the South were removed to the West. After that, things went on as before, until eventually the issue of slavery helped to precipitate a civil war which left the Blacks "free" but destitute, and the Indians about where they were. The Blacks immediately began a determined climb toward responsible participation in whatever was going on in America—a struggle not yet consummated but which as it nears fulfillment has opened the way for all others who have been discriminated against to make their bid for rectification.

It is inevitable that the Mexican Americans, *La Santa Raza*, should find themselves in the struggle. They are America's second largest minority, and they bear the traditional marks of the "outsider": poverty, political impotence, illiteracy, hopelessness, and immobility. These descendants of the Aztecs (who like the Indians have been romanticized in our literature but dismissed from our practical considerations) share with Black

Americans a common experience of being valued for their labor but not necessarily for themselves.

This is what this book is about. An award-winning journalist and a sociologist have combined their talents in order to chronicle the experience of Red, Brown, and Black Americans in their search for dignity and responsibility and for that modicum of power without which responsibility is a sham. The authors have delved into the reasons behind the Red, Brown, and Black power movements and have produced a highly readable account documenting accurately what these minority groups are and have been doing to confront the so-called establishment and discrimination throughout American society.

This is a great nation in potential. The Anglos, the Ethnics, the Black, the Red, and the Brown minorities have together made it so. But America can never reach her full potential until her claim to be one people rests on something more solid than the expectation that privilege and poverty will find their natural and proper distribution on the basis of race or color or ethnic origin. The era of ethnic and racial derogation is past. The "Hunkies," the "Micks," the "Spics," the "Kikes," the "Dagoes," the "Niggers," the "Redskins," and the "Wetbacks" don't know who they are anymore—and it is hard to keep somebody in "his place" if he doesn't know who you're talking about.

C. Eric Lincoln
Kumasi Hill
Antioch, Tennessee

Introduction

AS THE SEVENTIES settled over our nation in the wake of a decade of violence and civil unrest, a period of calm seemed to quell the storms of social protest. The sixties had raged impetuously against time-worn traditions which had kept millions of people in bondage. Assassinations, race riots, and mass demonstrations had errupted with a frequency which was staggering, and it seemed for a time as if the United States would disintegrate into total anarchy.

We lived through that era and are greater for the experience. When the sixties had dawned, minority people could expect little more than a life of second-class citizenship and a nearly impenetrable tangle of economic and social inequities. As the seventies opened, many of the social and economic obstacles had been destroyed and life for a minority person held at least the glimmer of hope.

The reason for this hope was that minority people had banded together to confront those institutions which had kept them imprisoned and had denied them the fruits of the free-enterprise system. This denial was, and is, one of our country's greatest shames. And it is to the credit of minority people that they challenged White America's institutions. For it was this challenge—at times bloody and terrifying—which forced open the doors to social equality long closed to people of color.

During the early sixties, poverty gripped a substantial percentage of the nation's population. [1] Many unfortunate Ameri-

---

[1] A consensus of figures released by various agencies during the mid and

11

cans faced starvation, lived in squalid, over-crowded living quar-ters, and received inadequate educations. In comparison to what John Kenneth Galbraith had termed the "affluent society," the nation's poor had fewer job opportunities, suffered more dis-ease and mental illness, had shorter life spans, were victimized by more crimes, experienced higher rates of divorce, separation, and desertion, and endured more intense feelings of worthless-ness, apathy, insecurity, and frustration.

Nearly half of the nation's nonwhite population subsisted below the poverty level. Of the 800,000 American Indians in the United States, upwards of eighty percent lived in poverty. Over half of the nation's Spanish-speaking citizens were pov-erty-ridden. And with the nation's largest minority group, the blacks, the situation remained grim. Seventy-five percent of all black people in the United States lived in urban slums, and a third of those (over five million) lived in abject poverty with incomes failing to meet the minimum daily needs established by the Social Security Administration.[2]

In an increasingly complex age, much of this rural and urban poverty went unseen. Government priorities were placed elsewhere, and Middle America—following the migration to the suburbs—directed most of its attention and material resources to suburbia. That placed the nation's poor in a peculiar situa-tion. Although White America—Middle America—voiced con-cern for racially designated minority groups, it placed responsi-bility for achievement on the poor. The Protestant Work Ethic placed great value upon employment—in essence, it measured a man's worth by his work. In the same vein, the Horatio Alger myth said that anyone could "pull himself up by his boot-straps" and make it.

---

early 1960's revealed that approximately 33 million Americans lived below the poverty level—that being the minimum income a family of four could subsist on without aid. Although figures varied among agencies—and now are obsolete—it could be said that early in the 1960's, that income figure was around $3,000 per year. At the close of that period, the figure had risen to about $3,700. These figures, of course, are to be taken as averages. [2]The interested reader can consult Michael Harrington's *The Other Ameri-ca* (New York: Macmillan, 1964) for a vivid description of poverty during the early sixties. For the mid and latter sixties, the *Report of the National Advisory Commission on Civil Disorders* (New York: Bantam Books, 1968) gives a good statistical breakdown of nonwhite poverty.

Without question, most Americans did achieve. But what about members of minority groups? The simple truth was that historically they had not achieved. In fact, they had been hindered from achieving by the very institutions which had propelled White Anglo-Saxon Protestant Americans into a condition of affluence unparalleled in the history of the world.

In 1969 the Michigan-Ohio Regional Educational Laboratory, a Detroit-based federal study project studying racism and its effects upon the United States, concluded that racism blocked nonwhite aspirations on all fronts—personal, social, cultural, economic, and political—and it placed most of the blame upon American institutions operating insidiously and invisibly to keep nonwhites subservient.[3]

Institutions have established laws, customs, systems of reward and punishment, and methods which affect the attitudes, beliefs, and behavior of the larger society. They can be defined as "fairly stable social arrangements and practices through which collective actions are taken."[4] For example, business as an institution has traditionally perpetuated certain concepts we came to accept as the American way of life. Ideas such as work being proof of a man's worth, the greatness of the free-enterprise system, and the Horatio Alger myth became American values. Consequently, we came to believe that a man must work; more important, he must know *how* to work. If a man's early environment failed to stress the work incentive and he was unable to perform in a job situation, we tended to regard him as lazy, of no account, or as something different and undesirable in our society.[5]

[3]Alan Hurwitz and Valerie Snook, *Pilot Study: Unit on White Racism,* Michigan-Ohio Regional Educational Laboratory, 3750 Woodward Ave., Detroit, Michigan, July, 1969, pp. 1-9.

[4]*Institutional Racism in American Society: A Primer,* Mid-Peninsula Christian Ministry Community House (East Palo Alto, California, April 15, 1968), pp. 2-3.

[5]Several observers suggest that this has changed. Dr. Robert J. Havighurst of the University of Chicago sees "work as a major source of self-respect" to be a receding value in American society. In his paper "The Values of Youth," Project on Student Values, August 8, 1968, he says: "A considerable fraction, both urban and rural, have deflated the value of work and have based their sense of self-respect upon other characteristics" (p. 7).

Grace Halsell, a white journalist who turned her skin black and went to live in Harlem and Mississippi, made an eloquent comment in her book *Soul Sister* about another institution— mass media. Describing her reaction to television, she said:

> As a black woman seated among black women, clustered around a T.V. set, it strikes me as strange, even idiotic, that all thoughts emanating from the screen are white-oriented, as if all other people, the people who don't have white skin, are not really out there in the audience. One woman on the screen claims that if she had her life to live over again, she'd live it as a blonde; and then she asks, "Wouldn't you really rather be blonde."[6]

Historically, business, mass media, education, religion, government, and other institutions acted collectively, brainwashing the masses of whites into a belief in racial and social superiority. Abraham F. Citron in "The Rightness of Whiteness" explained: "As a white child grows, he gradually assumes an unconscious feeling of white dominance. He orients himself in a white-centric world. The white self is felt as the human norm, the right, against which all persons of other color may be judged."[7]

Thus, the belief in racial superiority reinforced by institutional indoctrination inculcated itself within our white culture. In education we used white-oriented textbooks. Our IQ tests and other standardized measuring devices were designed for the experiences and vocabulary of the white middle-class child. We taught white middle-class values. In religion, we used white-oriented symbols of our faith and sent missionaries around the world to convert nonwhite "heathens." In other areas, mass media answered white needs for entertainment, government represented the white interests of the dominant society, and business served the white consumer.

These institutional activities, which acted to prejudice white society towards the view that being white in a White America was the normal and preferred way to be, had severe consequences. First, the rewards institutions had the power to dispense—education, career opportunities, political influence, fair

[6]Grace Halsell, *Soul Sister* (Cleveland: World, 1969), p. 74.
[7]Abraham F. Citron, "The Rightness of Whiteness," Inter-Cultural Center, Wayne State University, January, 1969, p. 1.

treatment by law, self-respect, and security—went almost exclusively to the segment of society those institutions served. Second, nonwhite minorities, under the influence of this institutional prejudice, themselves developed unconscious attitudes of inferiority.

Minority children were placed in the position of seeing that their parents traditionally had little power or status. Often they saw the world outside their ghetto or neighborhood via television, which showed them a white world with white models of success. In magazines, newspapers, movies, school textbooks, and other educational material, they saw their own group either ignored or portrayed in subservient, marginal, or distressed roles. All this worked to erode the aspirations and confidence of the nonwhite child. He was at a psychological disadvantage in competing with white children and too often gave up, reinforcing both his own sense of inadequacy and white society's estimate of him as inferior.

The evolution of our institutions into perpetuators of the concept of white supremacy can be seen as a natural and predictable process. Initially, an institution reflects the attitudes and needs of those it serves. But inevitably in time it ceases being servant and becomes master, it ceases reflecting attitudes and begins forming values. This had occurred in American society, and it was to this phenomenon that minority groups had to address themselves.

The power movements which evolved in the early sixties were responses to the power held by American institutions. They started with black people and spread to Chicanos and Indians. They started as reactions against poverty and the powerlessness of poverty and soon grew to encompass nearly every phase of minority life. This book is a guide to understanding the power movements of three minority groups—the Afro-American, the Mexican American, and the American Indian. Included are brief sections on important leaders and organizations within each minority group. And because no study of either a minority group or a power movement can be complete without some account of historical background, historical sketches have also been included in this work.

This, then, is a guide to understanding minority groups; but, more important, it is a guide to understanding the experience of minority groups in America.

PART ONE
BLACK POWER:

THE BLACK EXPERIENCE
IN AMERICA

1

BLACK POWER

THE POTPOURRI OF MISUNDERSTANDING

IN JULY OF 1966, a young black leader stood before a rally in Greenwood, Mississippi, and uttered a phrase that echoed around the world. Waves of indignation, anger, fear, and hope spread through the American people. Many saw blacks and whites rushing headlong into a bloody civil war. Others felt that blacks were pushing too hard. As a middle-aged, white New Yorker voiced it on one of the network news programs: "I've got nothing against them, but they've got to slow down. These things take time to heal." Segments of the population felt a vague uneasiness and marched out to buy guns, while a smaller segment who already owned guns loaded them and waited. Black people, trapped in the squalor of urban ghettos, smiled inwardly and nodded agreement, while still other black people shook their heads and thought, "slow down, brother." A few blacks loaded their guns and waited. The phrase that militant young leader coined in Greenwood was "Black Power." Stokely Carmichael, while addressing a gathering of marchers, cried out: "The only way we gonna stop them white men from whuppin' us is to take over. We been saying freedom for six years and we ain't got nothin'. What we gonna start saying now is black power."[1]

[1]Bradford Chambers, "Snick and 'Black Power': 1966," *Chronicles of Black Protest* (New York: Mentor Books, 1968), p. 216.

In the wake of that July afternoon the term "Black Power" sparked a landslide of controversy. Militants used it as a rallying point to unify their people—yet bigots claimed it was racism in reverse. It urged a more intensive search by the Afro-American into his past—yet the press toyed with words like "Black Supremacy." It told of a new black man, proud and determined—yet many resented its message. It chronicled a new movement, a movement by the black man to lift his race from poverty and despair, a movement with a message so strong and yet so simple that it spilled over into the camps of other minority groups. Perhaps no other phrase in modern social history has generated as much emotion, confusion, and misunderstanding. Simply stated, Black Power means that black people lift the black race out of the black man's hell. As a philosophy, it is the principle of self-determination, of the black man saying to White America, "I will do it," instead of, "You do it for me." As a reality, the concept of Black Power is a viable alternative to the twin-evils plaguing most minority groups— second-class citizenship and cultures which stress failure instead of success.

On April 4, 1968, an assassin's bullet struck down Dr. Martin Luther King, Jr. Dr. King's passing was more than the death of a great leader. It was also the death of a great movement—the Civil Rights Movement. From that day in history, black people in this country began taking a serious look at leaders like Stokely Carmichael and at philosophies like Black Power. Overnight, the black population matured, seeming to realize that the days of freedom marches, sit-ins, and the arm-linked-in-arm solidarity with white liberals had passed. In the aftermath of Dr. King's death, the black man took a long, cold look at himself, at his gains, and at his relative position in respect to white society. Somehow in April of 1968 the once-radical concept of Black Power no longer appeared so radical. In fact, the avenues to equality advocated by a handful of militants, including Carmichael and the Student Non-violent Coordinating Committee, made sense. Black Power had a message for a disillusioned Black Nation. It had an answer for those black people who saw Dr. King's murder as the ultimate betrayal by White America. The message was simple. Militants were saying: "Enough of turning the other cheek. Enough of asking the white man for handouts." It was time to unite, to use the power of a united black voice to demand those rights and benefits that are the birthright of every white American.

From its inception, Black Power has stressed unity. A second, but equally important, emphasis has been nationalism. The culture of poverty which White America has historically imposed upon most minority groups tends to corrode the image a minority group holds of itself. In other words, poverty implies inferiority and, as one militant voiced it, "If you tell a man he's inferior long enough, he's gonna start believing it." Although many minority groups have been able to overcome this attitude—either through especially strong ethnic ties or by merging with the dominate society—in the case of blacks, as well as Chicanos and Indians, this social and cultural "inferiority complex" has been quite virulent. Black Power seeks to reverse this.

BLACK POWER DEFINED

In the late sixties, Black Power was a movement at the grass-roots level to liberate Black Americans from poverty and failure. It stressed self-pride and unity—not violence—as a means to bring about equality. It directed black people to take a hard look at themselves and at their communities. It said black people must see what they are and what they have been. It urged them to seek out their history—both American and African—and recognize their heritage. It encouraged black people to redefine themselves, rejecting the stereotypes of laziness and immorality, and assert a positive self-image.[2] It stressed a sense of community, urging black people to become "soul brothers," to recognize their common heritage, their common needs and aspirations, and to work together towards common goals. For only by working together could black people have the strength and power to sway the political, social, and economic institutions which shaped and controlled their lives. The term Black Power did not necessarily mean Black Nationalism. Rather, it expressed the determination of black Americans to share in the responsibility of making the decisions which affected them. And Black Power accepted the proposition that "Black is

[2]Stokely Carmichael and Charles V. Hamilton, *Black Power: The Politics of Liberation in America* (New York: Vintage Books, 1967), pp. 37-39.

Beautiful," a proposition black people felt should be meaningful for all Americans.

THE BLACK HERITAGE

At the height of the Black Power Movement, black students on campuses across the nation were demanding and getting courses in Black Studies. In the inner-city, black residents demanded an equal voice in city government and the operation of schools. Black actors and models suddenly appeared in television commercials and magazine advertisements. Sidney Portier replaced the shuffling, wide-eyed Negro actors of the thirties and forties, and in comedy Dick Gregory broke the barrier against interracial sarcasm. Afro hairdos, black arm bands, denim jeans and jackets, dashikas, and youth standing tall and straight proclaiming their blackness became Black Power's external symbols. Internally, the belief that *black is beautiful* replaced the belief that black meant inferiority and second-class citizenship.

The new image was one of the black man looking at himself through different eyes—his own. As a Detroit militant said:

> The white slavemaster taught us our name. We were niggers, coons, darkies, and Sambos. He gave us our identity, and we believed him because he was the authority. He taught us that we were lazy, shiftless, sexually aggressive, irresponsible, and of no account. In a totalitarian system as efficient and brutal as Hitler's or Stalin's, he ground it into us that we were an inferior race of people. And we believed him. We believed him for 300 years, but we don't believe him any longer. We're defining ourselves now. We're discovering what we're all about, and what we're discovering is that we are an intelligent, beautiful race of people.[3]

Although many white people felt threatened by the new black image, the imagined race war never erupted. Black Power was, and is, a movement of nationalism, not of chauvinism. The rhetoric of Black Power was not saying black is better. It was

[3]This quote came from an interview with Anna Marie Hayes, Research Analyst for the Michigan-Ohio Regional Educational Laboratory. Although Mrs. Hayes is from Detroit, the interview was conducted in Lansing, Michigan, February 8, 1969.

saying that black was beautiful, as white was beautiful, as brown, yellow, and red were beautiful. It was asserting the dignity and brotherhood of all men.

THE ECONOMICS OF BLACK POWER

Economically, the Black Power philosophy urged black consumers to use their purchasing power to benefit black-owned businesses. Resembling the "Spend your money where you can work!" campaigns of the Great Depression, Black Power hoped to keep the spending dollar within the black community rather than losing it to suburban shopping centers and white-owned businesses. This principle, combined with government pressure to free small-business loans, was aimed at creating a new black entrepreneur class. The creation of black-owned businesses, Black Power explained, leads to the creation of new job markets for the black worker and, ultimately, to a rise in the standard of living within the black community. Often called Black Capitalism, this philosophy was based on the concept that economic power yields political and social power.[4]

THE POLITICS OF POWER

In the decade of the sixties, Black Americans stepped into a new arena, politics. In Massachusetts voters sent a tall, handsome black named Edward Brooke to Congress. In Cleveland an urbane, precise-speaking Carl Stokes was elected mayor. A state away, Richard Hatcher became mayor of Gary, Indiana. Even in the South, long the stronghold of white politicians, blacks were trying out new roles as paid public servants—as sheriffs, county officials, and councilmen. Blacks elected Charles Evers mayor of Fayette, Mississippi, and Julian Bond the representative from Georgia. Suddenly, the black vote was being recognized as a powerful force in determining a politician's future. It had elected John F. Kennedy in 1960, and in 1968 nearly cost Richard M. Nixon the presidency, threatening to send the election into the House of Representatives. Blacks were learning how to use their voting power, which represented nearly twenty

[4]Robert Goldston, *The Negro Revolution* (New York: Macmillan, 1968), p. 225.

percent of the voting strength of the principal Northern cities. At the very heart of this was the concept of Black Power.

Black power urged blacks to combine their voting strength and use it as a tool to pry open closed doors and bring needed improvements into the black community. From local to national issues, it told black people to unite and form a political power base. "Only from a position of power," said one leader, "can we get the government to listen. The government is powerful, and one man speaking up to it will be ignored. But 22-million speaking, and that government is going to sit up and pay attention."[5]

THE POWER OF BLACK POWER

The philosophy of Black Power was a beacon for the Black Nation after the Civil Rights Movement had awakened White America's conscience. It was a tool, and still is, especially for other minority groups. But more important, it represented a powerful new way for the black man to see himself, for as a philosophy Black Power offers human dignity and self-respect. As black people began implementing the tactics of unity and self-determination, other minority groups watched silently for signs of success or failure. When it became evident that the philosophy worked, the Mexican Americans, and later the American Indians, grimly set about the task of combatting the white power structure with this new weapon—which was not new at all, but had merely been misplaced in the struggle for survival.

The emergence of Black Power was not a sudden genesis. It had its roots in the more than 300 years of black experience in America, an experience which began with slavery.

[5]Mr. Henry Haygood, Research Analyst, Michigan-Ohio Regional Educational Laboratory. Interview in Lansing, Mich., Feb. 9, 1969.

2

THE BLACK EXPERIENCE IN AMERICA

SLAVERY

THE UGLIEST STORY in the history of the United States began in August, 1619, when twenty Africans stumbled down the gangplank of a Dutch man-of-war into Jamestown, England's first permanent settlement in the New World. Ironically, these first Africans came not as slaves, but as indentured servants, who after working their period of indenture were freed and given the same civil rights as their European counterparts. William Tucker, the first Negro born in British America, in 1624, was born a free man. However, other Africans would come. Soon there would be hundreds, and thousands, and tens of thousands, and eventually millions; but the others would come not as indentured servants but as slaves, as slaves in one of the most efficient systems of slavery ever recorded by man. They would come as history's greatest migration. They would come as chattel across the Atlantic; and for every two snatched from the African continent, only one would survive to labor under a white owner.

The institution of slavery is as old as man himself. Every ancient civilization of which we have records knew slavery. One of the three Babylonian social classifications was a slave class. Ancient Judeans had laws legalizing the keeping of slaves taken not only from other nations but from among themselves. Armies of slaves maintained the Egyptian social order. They built the Great Pyramid and the Sphinx of Khafre. The Greeks and Romans kept slaves. In fact, slavery was so common in the ancient world it prompted Plato to suggest that every man had the blood of many slaves in his veins.[6]

The commercial African slave trade began in 1444 when a Portuguese ship unloaded a consignment of African slaves at Lisbon. During the 400 years that followed, nearly forty million Africans were removed from their homeland and exported to Europe and the New World. Slaving was big business. It moved European nations to engage in fierce competition and made fortunes for slavers from all nations. Piracy on the high seas, violence, torture, and murder were all an integral part of the trade. It made men callous and cruel; it cost the lives of thousands of slavers and millions of slaves; and it wrought havoc on much of African native society.

The coast of Africa was called the "white man's grave," but the phrase cannot adequately describe the horror of the slave trade for the African natives. Chained neck to neck on long caravans, they were marched barefooted and naked to the coast, sometimes for distances of 500 miles. Some had been kidnapped. Some were criminals sold to the slavers by tribal chieftains. Others had been sold into slavery by their own families because of famine. Most were prisoners of native wars. On the coast, they were herded into large stockades called "barracoons" and examined by surgeons who discarded the old and the diseased. Those remaining were bargained for by representatives of slave companies. When the bargaining concluded, the representatives branded the slaves they had purchased and transported them in long canoes to the slave ships.

The actual ocean voyage, the "middle passage," generally lasted from six to ten weeks. Slaves were shackled two by two and packed into the ship's hold. It was not unusual for 500 men, women, and children to be stuffed into a space affording little more than twenty inches of headroom. Many of the slaves were unable to sit up or move more than a few inches during the entire voyage. They lived in their own excrement, and ventila-

---

[6]Lerone Bennett, Jr., *Before the Mayflower: A History of the Negro in America* (Baltimore: Penguin Books, 1962), p. 33.

tion was limited to whatever air filtered through the grids above the hold. Food usually consisted of a rice or corn gruel. When a slave refused to eat, as was often the case, his teeth might be broken and the gruel poured down his throat. Entertainment often took the form of forced singing or, if room permitted, forced dancing.

The African's alternatives to submission were rebellion or suicide. Historians have recorded a few successful slave revolts, but in most instances the ship's crew put down rebellions swiftly and efficiently. Suicide presented a more difficult problem. Many of the slaves believed they had been abducted to feed a race of giant cannibals. This, plus the unbearable conditions aboard ship, drove countless slaves to suicide. It was common practice for ship's captains to order special nets rigged around their vessels to catch slaves leaping overboard. Other preventive measures were suicide watches, daily inspections of living quarters, and ceremonies like "dancing the slaves," the crew forcing the slaves to hop around to the accompaniment of fiddle music, thus exhausting them and keeping them too preoccupied to consider suicide. Despite every precaution, however, a few slaves on each voyage managed suicide, many by suffocating themselves or by driving nails through their own brains.

Disease was the scourge of slave trading. Very few ships reached ports in the New World without at least one incident of smallpox or flux.[7] Other diseases like yellow fever, leprosy, and elephantiasis stalked the slave trade with the same relentless determination as the ever-present schools of sharks that trailed the vessels across the Atlantic. The only real precaution taken by slavers against disease was removal. As soon as a slave displayed the symptoms of an epidemic disease, the captain ordered him thrown overboard.

When the slave ship finally put into port in the New World, those slaves who had managed to survive capture and middle passage were sold. Then began an intense training period, lasting

---

[7]John Hope Franklin, *From Slavery to Freedom: A History of Negro Americans* (New York: Vintage Books, 1947), p. 56.

anywhere from three months to three years, in which the slave learned pidgin English, was broken to discipline ("tamed"), and acquired the essential skills of whatever his occupation would be.

The consignment of slaves that landed in Jamestown in 1619 were not the first black men in the New World. Spanish-controlled regions had been importing Africans as slaves for almost a century before. Prior to this, Negroes had accompanied the earliest explorers to the New World. Many historians now believe that Columbus' pilot, Pedro Alonso Ninoas, was a black man. Balboa took thirty Negroes with him when he discovered the Pacific Ocean. Estevanico, a black explorer, opened New Mexico and Arizona for the Spaniards. Negroes went into Peru with Pizarro, and into Mexico with Cortez. They participated in the French explorations of Canada, and aided Jesuits in their first attempts at establishing missions in the New World. What the twenty Africans unloaded at Jamestown represent is a measurable starting point for the black slave trade in the America destined to become the United States.

The early British colonies were business ventures operating with permission and encouragement from the Crown. For example, Jamestown was established and financed by a private corporation, the Virginia Company. The colonies produced trade goods such as tobacco, sugar, rice, pitch, tar, turpentine, and cedar board and exported them to the company for sale throughout Europe. Being a business venture, the colonies had to produce enough goods to make a satisfactory profit for the board of directors. And the amount of goods the colonies produced depended upon the labor supply at their disposal.

At first, the colonies tried to meet their labor needs by importing white indentured servants, but the supply did not meet the demand—not to mention the problem of having to replace an indentured servant every five or ten years when his period of indenture expired. The colonies needed a more abundant labor supply, conceivably of laborers who could be bonded for life.

There were a few early attempts at bonding white servants for life, but these attempts failed because British common law protected European bondsmen against involuntary enslavement.

When the colonists attempted to use Indian labor, they encountered other problems. Indians tended to sicken and die under slavery. The colonists finally turned their attention to the African.

From the experiences in the Spanish colonies, the American colonists knew that Africans were well suited to slavery. They were strong, durable—and highly visible. An African might escape, but unlike white slaves he could not avoid detection by blending into the crowd. Economically, one African cost about the same as an indentured servant and once purchased did not have to be replaced within a few years. And although British protection should have extended to the African, the colonists and the Royal governors overlooked that matter. Thus, the African represented a labor source bondable for life. Moreover, from the colonists' viewpoint there seemed to be an unlimited supply of the "dark-skinned heathens."

As there was a need for labor, there was an economic institution eager to fill that need. For a hundred years the European nations had competed with each other for control of the slave trade. Towards the end of the seventeenth century, England's powerful Royal Africa Company, with help from the British navy, gained control. Together with colonial traders, England virtually flooded the American colonies with African slaves. Only one problem remained—the morality of slavery itself.

As one institution supplied the slaves, another justified their use. To answer the slavery question the colonists called upon religion.[8] Because Africans were not Christians they were considered heathens, and heathens were regarded as something less than human. Any lingering doubts could quickly be dispelled by quoting the Bible. For example, Leviticus 25:44 states: "Both thy bondmen and thy bondmaids, which thou shalt have, shall be of the heathen that are around you; of them shall ye buy bondmen and bondmaids."

Slavery in America lasted for over 200 years. No one knows for sure when it started in practice, but court records allude to it in the early 1630's. Actual statutory recognition of the institution came in 1641 in Massachusetts' famous *Body of*

[8]Bennett, *Mayflower*, p. 37.

Liberties, which stated that no man could be bonded "unless it be laefull Captives taken in just warres, and such strangers as willingly sell themselves or are sold to us."[9] In 1661 and 1663, Virginia and Maryland passed laws enslaving Negroes for life, forbidding interracial marriages, and giving Negro children the status, free or bond, of their mother. A 1667 ruling by the Virginia Assembly shifted the justification for bondage from religion to race: "Baptisme doth not alter the condition of the person as to his bondage or freedom. . . ." [10]

By the middle of the eighteenth century, slavery had become a firmly established institution in the colonies. Tobacco and rice plantations existed in the South; the domestic slave trade flourished in Virginia; and forerunners of the infamous Black Codes existed in every colony having slave labor. On the other side, Quakers had denounced slavery as being inhuman and in·violation of God's will; and in the North abolitionist societies were forming. The mid-eighteenth century was also a time of reflection about that institution which had become so firmly entrenched, for the colonies were about to go to war with England for the freedom and equality of all mankind.

The institution of slavery was somewhat of an anomaly during the American Revolution. Much of the revolutionary philosophy was based on the work of the English philosopher John Locke. Locke had carefully explained that the nature of society was a contract between various people banded together for mutual benefit. He had pointed out that the rights of the people transcended the rights of the government and that chief among those rights were liberty, individualism, private property, and the equality of all men within that society. Many colonists were acutely aware that 500,000 Negroes were being held in bondage, denied even the recognition of being human.

In the years preceding the revolution Northerners had grown increasingly disenchanted with the institution of slavery. For one thing, it had not proven itself profitable in the early industrial structure of the North. For another, the question of morality was not so easily dismissed when there was no eco-

[9]Franklin, *Slavery to Freedom,* p. 101.
[10]August Meier and Elliot M. Rudwick, *From Plantation to Ghetto* (New York: Hill and Wang, 1966), p. 38.

nomic necessity for the institution. Colony after colony had attempted to halt or at least control the importation of slaves, but because slaving was big business, British policy consistently overruled their stands. Political radicals, both Northern and Southern, openly condemned slavery, and Thomas Jefferson even inserted a clause in the Declaration of Independence criticizing the King's slave-trading practices: "He had waged cruel war against human nature itself, violating its most sacred rights of life and liberty in the persons of a distant people who never offended him, captivating and carrying them into slavery in another hemisphere. . . ."[11] (The statement never reached the King because of opposition from a Southern delegation.) Thus, in pre-revolutionary America, slavery was very much on the minds of the English colonials, and every colony with the exception of South Carolina and Georgia agreed to consider abolition.

When the revolutionary fervor finally erupted in a Massachusetts colony on March 5, 1770, an ex-slave, Crispus Attucks, led a group of colonists against British soldiers. The event came to be known as the Boston Massacre, and the tall Negro leading the insurrection was killed. Negro blood was the first blood drawn in the cause for American independence. When the battles of Lexington and Concord blazed, Negroes took up arms with the minutemen against England. When British Major John Pitcairn cried in jubilation "The day is ours!" at the Battle of Bunker Hill, a Negro soldier named Peter Salem took aim and shot him dead.[12] Throughout the arduous war, Negroes fought alongside whites with determination and the same dedication to the ideals of freedom.

The American Revolution was not only a turning point for the English colonies, it was a turning point for American slavery. Many slaves received their freedom by serving in the armed forces. Many found freedom through postwar manumissions. Still others gained freedom when in 1787 the Continental Congress abolished slavery north of the Ohio River. Slavery became an institution confined to the South, and even there it looked for a time as if slavery might die for good.

In the late eighteenth century, Virginia, Maryland, and

[11]Goldston, *Negro Revolution*, p. 52.
[12]Franklin, *Slavery to Freedom*, p. 131.

North Carolina suffered a prolonged agricultural depression. Tobacco prices fell and crop sizes shrunk because of soil erosion. In these areas slavery became uneconomical and talk flourished over abolishing it. Then, when speculation reached its peak, an inventor named Eli Whitney constructed a simple machine in 1793 that separated the seed from cotton fiber. Cotton became big business. The cotton gin had sentenced Southern Negroes to another fifty years of slavery.

The last fifty years of slavery saw cotton assert itself as the core of the Southern economy. The Cotton Kingdom stretched over a thousand miles from South Carolina to Texas with nearly two million slaves producing three-quarters of the world's cotton supply. This was the land of the great plantations sometimes working hundreds of slaves (although the majority of plantations employed fewer than twenty). This was the land portrayed by *Uncle Tom's Cabin* and *Gone With the Wind*. This was the land of slavery's most oppressive moment.

The average slave lived in a one-room shack constructed of clapboard or logs. The roof generally leaked and the wind blew through numerous cracks in the walls. The shacks had dirt floors, no windows, and very little furniture.[13] The average annual clothing allowance for a man consisted of two cotton shirts, two woolen trousers, and one woolen jacket issued in the fall, and two cotton shirts and two cotton trousers issued in the spring. Masters usually issued one pair of shoes a year and a woolen blanket every third year. Women received eight to ten yards of cloth twice a year and wore the same style of shoe as the man. The average food allowance for each adult slave consisted of a peck of corn and four pounds of salt pork each week. Children received a fractional portion of the adult ration.[14] The workday lasted from sunup to sundown, except during harvest time when the day was extended. On most plantations, masters honored Sunday as the day off. A few plantations also allowed a half-day on Saturday.

The slave was regarded by law as property. He had no legal standing in the courts, could offer no testimony except against

13*Ibid.*, p. 195.
14Bennett, *Mayflower*, pp. 72-73.

other Negroes, could make no contracts or own property. His marriages were not recognized by law. Each slave was taught to consider himself inferior to any white man, and he had to obey every white man without question. He was forbidden to hit a white person, even in self-defense. These Black Codes, as they came to be known, encompassed practically every phase of the slave's life. In addition, they forbade the slave to leave his plantation without written permission, to assemble without a white person present, to visit homes of white acquaintances or free Negroes, to have firearms, or even in some areas to beat a drum.

Slavery was so dismal for the Negro that many mothers smothered their infants rather than have them grow up as slaves. Others tried to escape through the Underground Railroad to the North, or into the swamps, where they lived off the land, raiding nearby plantations for supplies. The majority of slaves turned to religion for deliverance and the hope of a better life in the hereafter. A few slaves revolted.

On August 30, 1800, Gabriel Prosser gathered a thousand slaves six miles from Richmond, Virginia. Only a severe thunderstorm which washed out the roads and bridges prevented him from attacking. Forced to postpone his insurrection, he was caught a few days later and hanged. In 1811 federal and state troops had to put down a rebellion of four hundred slaves in Louisiana. In 1821 authorities caught and hanged Denmark Vesey, who had recruited nine thousand slaves for a revolution in Charleston, South Carolina. And in 1831, Nat Turner led a revolt in Southampton County, Virginia, which left fifty-seven whites dead. All totaled, historians have uncovered over 250 slave revolts and conspiracies. So numerous were the rumors of proposed uprisings that white slaveowners lived in constant dread, and white slave patrols were maintained to continually search Negro cabins and to patrol roads and pathways for any hint of a conspiracy.

Slavery in the South has often been termed the *peculiar institution*. It dominated the Old South, but only a fourth of the white population owned slaves. It kept a large number of whites poor because it removed the need for a labor class, yet poor whites were among its greatest advocates. It placed the

Southern economy on a precarious foundation, and yet plantation owners clung tenaciously to "King Cotton." Perhaps because it was such a peculiar institution, it had to crumble.

JIM CROW

The decade immediately following the Civil War was a
period of hope for the American Negro. The slave had been
freed, granted citizenship, and enfranchised. In many areas of
the South, Negroes ate where they pleased, walked the streets
arm-in-arm with white friends, rode next to whites in streetcars
and on trains, and held political office. Negro writers of this
period frequently commented that their treatment in the postwar South far surpassed that in their native New York or New
England. Congress, through its Reconstruction policies, seemed
intent upon securing full rights forever for the freedmen; and
even if millions of ex-slaves were left penniless, largely unedu-
cated, and confused by the sudden change in social order, they
at least held hope for their fabled "forty acres and a mule." [15]
The story of Jim Crow began in 1877 when the federal troops
evacuated the South, leaving the fate of the Negro in the hands
of Southern whites.

The system of segregation called "Jim Crow" was a new
phenomenon in the South. Under slavery, whites and Negroes
had lived on fairly intimate terms, although whites had clearly
and often brutally reminded the Negro of his inferior status. On
smaller farms, for example, master and slave had worked side by
side in the fields, and they had often shared the same or at least
nearby quarters. Segregation actually had its start in the Northern states, where steamboats, passenger trains, streetcars, restaurants, and hotels were typical agencies of discrimination. [16]
Separation of the races in the South was a gradual process, not
fully completed until the twentieth century.

The first step in this process occurred when Southern whites
took the power of the ballot box away from Negroes. Disen-

[15] A popular rumor existed among the freedmen that the government
planned to divide the great plantations into forty-acre parcels and award
these parcels, with a mule to work the land, to the freedmen.
[16] C. Vann Woodward, The Strange Career of Jim Crow (New York:
Oxford University, 1966), p. 17.

franchisement was accomplished in a number of ways. Whites frequently moved polling places without notifying Negroes; they established poll taxes, property requirements, and literacy tests; they used violence and threats of violence. But probably the most effective tool in disenfranchising the Negro was the use of the "grandfather clause," which allowed no one to vote unless his father or grandfather had been able to vote on a certain day—such as January 1, 1860, when Negroes had been unable to vote anywhere in the South.

With their political power stripped away, Negroes sought help from the courts. However, in one decision after another the Supreme Court ruled against the Negro. In the 1876 ruling of the *United States v. Cruikshank,* the Court said regarding the Fourteenth Amendment that the federal government could not lawfully protect Negroes against discrimination by private individuals. A few years later the Court found the Civil Rights Act of 1875 unconstitutional. In the 1896 landmark decision in *Plessy v. Ferguson,* the Court legalized "separate but equal" facilities. Two years later, in *Williams v. Mississippi,* the Court upheld disenfranchisement by approving the use of poll taxes, literacy tests, and residential requirements. These cases and others like them not only rendered the Southern Negro politically impotent, they removed legal protection, leaving him to the mercy of white extremists and bigots. Jim Crow laws sprang up throughout the South.

Jim Crow laws forbade Negroes to be on the streets after a certain time. Negroes could not intermarry with whites. Public facilities were strictly segregated (some areas even specified the kind of paint and size of letters that could be used for the words WHITE and COLORED). Black patients could not be attended by white nurses or vice versa. In Birmingham, Alabama, Negroes could not play checkers with whites. In South Carolina, they were forbidden to look out the same windows whites had used. White and Negro prostitutes were segregated into separate districts in New Orleans. And in court Negroes took the oath using separate Jim Crow Bibles.

As there was a Jim Crow by law, there was also a Jim Crow by custom. Black men were forbidden to look at white women, on penalty of death; yet an attractive black woman found herself subject to the will of white men. If a Negro struck a white, even in self-defense, he could expect a lynching party at his cabin door, while a white could murder a Negro without fear of reprisal. Negroes were required to show proper respect to whites, and severe were the penalties for being "uppity." Negroes had to step off the sidewalk when whites passed. They had to use the words *sir* and *m'am* when addressing whites. They were forbidden to work except at the most menial jobs, constituting that class of laborers "last hired and first fired." To insure obedience to these codes, Southern extremists conducted a system of terror and vigilante reprisal.

In the ten-year period following 1889, whites lynched an average of 187 Negroes per year. From 1900 to the start of World War I, over 1,100 Negroes met the same fate.[17] This era constituted the darkest hour for the emancipated Negro, and even the voice of Booker T. Washington, America's most influential black leader of this period, failed to halt terrorist groups like the Ku Klux Klan. Denied his civil as well as his human rights, the Negro was powerless to stop the vicious attacks against his race. And the attacks were many.

A murder trial in Statesboro, Georgia, in 1904 ended in mass terrorism. The two convicted Negroes were pulled from the court and burned alive by a white mob. The mob then ran wild attacking other Negroes, including the mother of a three-day-old infant. They beat the woman with fists and clubs until she fell, whereupon they began kicking her in the face and ribs. When the woman's husband tried to protest, the crowd turned on him, beating him to death. Two years later, in Brownsville, Georgia, whites exploded into racial fury after being stirred up by a local newspaper. They moved through the Negro section burning houses and attacking blacks on sight. Police fired into groups of Negroes trying to defend themselves. Four prominent blacks were murdered and scores injured. In another gruesome incident, a white mob in Texas bound the hands and feet of a black man and set upon him with clubs. Shortly thereafter, as he laid groaning, they threw him into a fire. Men, women, and children gathered around the blaze and laughed and taunted the screaming man until he died. The spectators then pulled his

17Franklin, *Slavery to Freedom,* p. 439.

body from the flames and cut off chunks of burned flesh, carrying them home for souvenirs. Violence was everywhere, and not only in the South.

Springfield, Ohio, was the scene of a racial incident in 1904. A group of white citizens broke into the city jail and murdered a Negro implicated in the death of his employer. The crowd hung the man's body from a pole and pumped it full of bullets. Afterwards, they vented their hatred of the city's Negro population by burning homes and shops. Four years later, in August of 1908, another riot erupted in Springfield, Illinois. A white woman in Springfield accused a Negro of raping her. Before a grand jury, however, she admitted that she had actually been assaulted by a white man. Nevertheless, the city's white population had worked itself into such a frenzy that they raided stores, stealing guns and axes, and began destroying Negro businesses and homes. They lynched a Negro barber behind his burned shop and dragged his body through the streets. Later they pulled an eighty-four-year-old Negro from his home and lynched him a block from the State House.[18]

At the turn of the century, the Southern Negro found himself locked into a system affording him little more than he had known under slavery. His political power had been stripped away; his job prospects had been narrowed to sharecropping, tenant-farming, or only the most menial labor, assuring him a life of poverty; and his social environment had deteriorated to a state of degradation and fear. Alarmed by these conditions, W.E.B. DuBois called a meeting of Negro leaders and intellectuals during the summer of 1905.

William Edward Burghardt DuBois had been the first Negro to receive a Ph.D. from Harvard. He was a historian of considerable scholarship, and his doctoral dissertation *The Suppression of the African Slave Trade* became the first published work in the Harvard Historical Studies series. When he called together the Negro leaders in 1905, he did so from the belief that the American Negro could not afford to wait for the white society

[18]Details on riots and other incidents in Statesboro, Brownsville, and Springfield drawn from Franklin, *Slavery to Freedom*, pp. 440-444.

to bestow equality. His research into history had pointed to one constantly recurring conclusion that oppressors do not willingly free the oppressed.

The meeting was held at Niagara Falls, Canada, and the leaders who had attended formed the Niagara Movement, which demanded of white society an end to racial discrimination and the acceptance of the principles of brotherhood. However, from the start the fledgling organization ran into problems. Booker T. Washington, the most prominent Negro leader at the time, was not a member but continued to draw the bulk of white financial contributions, drawing away funds desperately needed by the Movement. A second problem was the organization itself. The Niagara Movement was considered by many Negroes, as well as whites, too radical for support. Within five years of its founding, the Movement disbanded, but its short life helped spawn another organization.

On February 12, 1909, Lincoln's birthday, the Niagara leaders accepted an invitation to attend a meeting with a group of prominent whites in New York City. The meeting had been called by Oswald Garrison Villard, grandson of William Lloyd Garrison, to discuss the condition of the American Negro and to explore ways of achieving political and civil equality. From this meeting, and another in May, 1910, the National Association for the Advancement of Colored People was born.

Immediately the new organization launched a series of legal battles to end segregation and discrimination. During the first fifteen years of its existence, the NAACP won three important decisions before the Supreme Court. In 1915 the "grandfather clauses" of Maryland and Oklahoma were declared unconstitutional; in a 1917 decision the Court ruled the housing ordinances of Louisville, Kentucky, unconstitutional; and in 1923 the Court ruled in a particular case that a Negro convicted of murder had not been given a fair trial because Negroes had been excluded from the jury. The NAACP represented new hope for the black man in America, but it took time, time and grueling work, to repair nearly 300 years of hatred. The first half of the twentieth century remained a nightmare of inequality and abuse.

THE CIVIL RIGHTS MOVEMENT

Each morning of every schoolday Oliver Brown of Topeka, Kansas, worried about his eight-year-old daughter Linda. For each morning of every schoolday she had to cross a railroad freightyard to catch a schoolbus that transported her and other black children twenty-one blocks to a segregated Negro school. Although the Kansas school systems generally provided equal facilities for white and black schools, Oliver Brown felt that segregation itself was harmful. A white school operated only five blocks from his home, yet his daughter was barred from attending it and forced to ride to a special school. Brown met with several other black parents, and early in 1951, with help from the NAACP, filed suit against the city of Topeka. Oliver Brown's case, together with four others from states bordering the deep South, constituted part of the NAACP's frontal attack against public school segregation. This attack began in 1950 and ended in 1954 when the Supreme Court ruled that the segregation of public schools by race violated the Fourteenth Amendment to the Constitution. Oliver Brown was an instrument of change—a part of the many changes affecting the United States since the end of World War II.

Postwar America was a new America of unprecedented growth and prosperity. Four years of working in the war industries, of decent wages and large blocs of overtime, of rationing and restraint in spending as goods went into the war effort had provided the American people with considerable spending capital. The Depression had passed, leaving most Amerians with a bitter aftertaste, but the Depression *had* passed. Industry converted to a consumer economy and increased production to meet the increased consumer demand. Soldiers returning from Europe and the Pacific returned to a new America of opportunity. Congress had passed a GI Bill of Rights and a college education no longer belonged solely to the rich. Social caste had died—for most Americans. Postwar America was also an America of anxiety. The Cold War had locked the two major powers in a grim game of political chess and the threat of nuclear holocaust haunted the nation. But holocaust or not, America continued to grow and prosper. Hospitals strained under the postwar "baby boom," and contractors struggled to meet the demands for new houses for the new families. America had truly become that fabled "land of milk and honey" as progress created a general feeling of well-being and economic security—for most.

Postwar America for the Negro was still the America of poverty, racial prejudice, segregation, violence, and second-class citizenship. By the time the United States had entered the Second World War, the Negro had already undergone a variety of experiences. World War I had lured millions of Southern Negroes northward to work in the war industries. They had settled in the urban centers of the major Northern cities, and as Negro sections had pushed out into white residential areas, tensions had mounted. A series of race riots accompanied the Great Migration of the First World War, culminating in the "Red Summer of 1919," when twenty-six racial conflagrations erupted. The most serious had occurred in Chicago, where a dispute over the drowning of a black youth touched off thirteen days of violence. When the militia finally gained control, the tally recorded thirty-eight persons dead and 537 injured.

The Red Summer of 1919 had seen moods of anger and despair sweep across the country, but right on its tail exploded the "roaring twenties." The twenties was a decade of speakeasies and hip flasks; of flappers, the Black Bottom, and the famed "tin lizzie"; of credit buying and prosperity; of speculation and a wildly soaring stock market that seemed perfectly willing to make fortunes for everyone—forever. On the surface the twenties seemed to offer a temporary truce from racial violence. In New York a group of highly talented Negro writers were busy forging a new identity for the black man. Claude McKay, Jean Toomer, Countee Cullen, Langston Hughes, and James Weldon Johnson turned the world's attention to Harlem and the *Harlem Renaissance*. But under the surface, in other parts of the country, the Ku Klux Klan had reappeared and was busy lynching not only blacks, but Catholics and Jews as well.

Out of the ecstasy and fear of the twenties came Marcus Garvey, a short, plump black Jamaican. In the name of Black Nationalism, he formed the Universal Negro Improvement Association, sponsoring a "back to Africa" movement. Garvey caught the imagination of millions of American Negroes, and thousands joined his movement. In 1927, however, the United States government deported him as an undesirable alien. Black America was shocked by the incident, the more so when it was revealed that the plucky Jamaican had been convicted of using the mails to defraud. Yet, the trauma was slight compared to the trauma of the stock market crash in 1929. When the Great Depression hit America, it hit the Negro the hardest. For the next decade and a half, Black America lived hand-to-mouth.

World War II ended the Depression, and postwar America saw more Negroes in the North as Southern Negroes, following a pattern established during the First World War, had journeyed north to work in the war industries. A few enjoyed the prosperity of the postwar years, but for most, the North was merely another kind of prison. Negro soldiers returning from Europe and the Pacific returned to the same America of Jim Crow, *de facto* segregation, and overt racism they had left. What was significant in postwar America was that the slightest sign of hope flickered through the despair.

Racial attitudes had begun to soften. The racial policies of Nazi Germany reminded many thoughtful whites of not dissimilar racial policies in the United States. In addition, the Negro migrations into the Northern urban centers had created a new source of political power. Northern politicians quickly recognized the importance of the Negro vote. Thirdly, the United States' participation in both the formation and operation of the United Nations tended to spotlight racial inequality in America. With the emergence of new nonwhite nations, this created diplomatic problems. Against this backdrop the NAACP carried on legislative battles for equality.

Prior to mid-century, the NAACP had concentrated on the aspect of *equality* in the "separate but equal" ruling of *Plessy v. Ferguson*. In 1950 it attacked segregation itself by challenging the constitutionality of public school segregation. On May 16 it filed suit in the federal court of South Carolina to end segregation in the schools of Clarendon County. One year later, on May 23, 1951, it filed a similar suit in Virginia after 450 Negro students had gone on strike in Prince Edward County. These and three other cases—Oliver Brown's from Topeka, another from Wilmington, Delaware, and a third from the District of Columbia—reached the Supreme Court's docket entitled *Oliver Brown et al. v. Board of Education of Topeka.*

In *Brown v. Board of Education* the NAACP lawyers argued that the institution of segregation, aside from violating the Fourteenth Amendment, damaged the mental growth of Negro children. The fact that segregation *implied* inferiority interfered with learning regardless of the adequacy of educational facilities. Furthermore, they continued, segregation heightened interracial tensions by obstructing communication between whites and blacks. In advancing its case, the NAACP brought in experts and introduced sociological and psychological studies proving that there existed no innate differences in intelligence between white and black children. On Monday, May 17, 1954, the Supreme Court answered by reversing the *Plessy v. Ferguson* decision of 1896, unanimously ruling that segregation by race in public schools was unconstitutional.

The Court's decision in *Brown v. Board of Education* met varied reactions. It was the most significant piece of legislation affecting the American Negro since the Emancipation Proclamation, and the North, as well as the World, applauded the verdict. Jim Crow was legally dead. The reaction of the border states to the south was somewhat less enthusiastic, but they complied and began quietly desegregating their schools. In the deep South, however, the general reaction was a fusion of alarm and outright resistance. Less than two months after "Black Monday" (the name given the day of the Supreme Court's ruling), the first White Citizens Council sprouted in Indianola, Mississippi. Soon Citizens Councils, operating through legal and quasi-legal channels to preserve the social order of the South, spread to every Southern state. These Citizens Councils saw as their prime task stopping integration in public schools, and they exerted their influence in numerous ways, from endorsing political candidates favoring segregation to levying economic reprisals against progressive Negroes and liberal whites. Yet, the White Citizens Councils, and even the Ku Klux Klan, could not prevent the seed of human rights which had been planted on "Black Monday" from germinating and burgeoning into a movement of twenty million Americans seeking their legal and civil rights.

The 1954 Brown decision set the stage for what later

became known as the Civil Rights Movement. It removed the legal barricades preventing Southern Negroes from securing their full rights under the law, and it represented a long step which ultimately rallied blacks and concerned whites across the nation to attack the evils of a Jim Crow system. In a manner of speaking, the Brown decision helped secure the "ammunition" for the Civil Rights Movement. The leader needed to direct that cause emerged the following year in Montgomery, Alabama.

On Thursday, December 1, 1955, Mrs. Rosa Parks, a forty-three-year-old Negro seamstress, boarded the Cleveland Avenue bus in downtown Montgomery. She was employed at the Montgomery Fair, a large department store, and after work she had gone shopping. On the segregated bus, she took the first seat behind the white section. She was tired from her long day and her feet ached. As the bus moved along its route, it gradually filled. When six white passengers boarded the full bus at the Empire Theatre stop, the driver turned around and ordered several Negroes, including Mrs. Parks, to give up their seats to the white passengers. Rosa Parks refused and was arrested on the spot.

Montgomery's Negro community was outraged by the incident. E.B. Nixon, an NAACP official, bailed Rosa Parks out of jail and promptly contacted the city's Negro leaders. At a special emergency meeting these leaders formed the Montgomery Improvement Association to coordinate a boycott of the bus line. They appointed the young pastor of the Dexter Avenue Baptist Church, the Reverend Martin Luther King, Jr., as president.

The Montgomery Bus Boycott lasted nearly thirteen months and ended when the bus line finally complied with a Supreme Court ruling to desegregate its buses. During its course, extremist whites bombed the homes of E.B. Nixon and Dr. King. Montgomery's Negroes were threatened, arrested, and in a few cases physically assaulted. However, from the start the Negro community held steadfastly to the philosophy of nonviolence which had been outlined by Dr. King at a rally preceding the boycott. A mixture of the teachings of Gandhi and Christ, nonviolence stressed the use of love as a weapon against hate.

The publicity accompanying the boycott lauded nonviolence and made Dr. King a celebrity. He became a popular guest speaker at sympathetic churches and colleges. Various organizations invited him to instruct them on the use of the boycott and nonviolence as a tactic against civil injustice. The NCAAP awarded him the Springarn Medal for an outstanding contribution to race relations, and *Time Magazine* ran a cover story on him. His name assumed national and international importance and his example stirred others into action. Similar boycotts broke out in Birmingham, Tuskegee, and Atlanta. The Montgomery Bus Boycott had illustrated the success of mass action, shifting the emphasis of Negro protest from the courtroom to the street.

Early in 1957, Dr. King met with clergy from ten Southern states and formed the Southern Christian Leadership Conference to coordinate the nonviolent movement that had been spreading since the Montgomery Bus Boycott. He was appointed president. Meanwhile, the federal government threw in its hat in favor of civil rights. On August 29, Congress passed the Civil Rights Act of 1957, which established a Civil Rights Commission to investigate and report on cases of racial discrimination at the polls. Though ineffective in the South, it constituted the first civil rights legislation passed in the twentieth century. One month later, the government demonstrated its willingness to protect the legal rights of the Negro when President Eisenhower ordered federal troops into the town of Little Rock, Arkansas, to carry out the planned integration of Central High School.

The Civil Rights Movement was still in its infancy during the late fifties, but already dominant themes were emerging. One, of course, was the principle of nonviolence, the "turn-the-other-cheek" philosophy which so effectively captured worldwide approval for the movement. A second theme was the use of public facilities, such as Montgomery's bus line, as concrete symbols of white abuse and racial inequality. Another theme, and one with explosive ramifications, was the unexpected commitment of youth to securing equality for all. When the sixties arrived, these themes seemed to reach maturity, initiating a movement which snowballed quickly past the point of no return and crashed headlong into the heart of Southern racism and demagoguery.

On February 1, 1960, four Negro students from North Carolina A & T College at Greensboro sat at a Woolworth lunch counter. When refused service because they were black, they remained in their seats until the store closed. The next day they returned; and the next; and the next, each time being joined by more students. Many observers feel that the Greensboro sit-in represents the formal starting point of the Civil Rights Movement. The sit-ins spilled into other North Carolina cities—Winston-Salem, Charlotte, Fayetteville—and into other states—Virginia, South Carolina, Tennessee, Alabama—until the movement had affected more than 100 cities in twenty different states and had involved more than 70,000 people. The sit-in idea had struck the imaginations of thousands of college students, and they were its most vigorous proponents. So enthusiastic was their response that a special organization, the Student Non-violent Coordinating Committee under the guidance of Dr. King, was formed to coordinate their forays.

As SNCC continued to direct sit-ins, another organization initiated an attack against segregation in Southern bus terminals. On May 4, 1961, a chartered bus carrying thirteen riders left Washington, D.C., bound for New Orleans. Sponsored by the Congress of Racial Equality and headed by James Farmer, six whites and seven blacks participated in this "freedom ride" into the South. The bus traveled through Virginia, North and South Carolina, and Georgia with little trouble. However, it met strong resistance in Alabama. A white mob attacked it at Anniston, setting fire to the bus with an incendiary bomb. Another bus carried the riders to Birmingham, where a second attack followed. Unable to charter a carrier out of Birmingham, the original group flew to New Orleans and disbanded, but the concept of the freedom ride did not end there. Three other civil rights organizations—SNCC, SCLC, and the Nashville Student Movement—decided to continue the rides. On May 20, a third bus of freedom riders left Birmingham for Montgomery. Upon arrival, they met an angry mob which attacked them and then turned on newsmen and Negro bystanders. Several hours of rioting followed, prompting Attorney General Robert Kennedy to dispatch federal marshalls to restore order. The following day, Alabama's governor John Patterson declared martial law.

The riders remained in Montgomery for four days. Dr. King,

cutting short a speaking tour, flew there to help calm the outraged Negro population. He was joined by James Farmer and other CORE officials. In a news conference Dr. King and Mr. Farmer announced their intention of completing the ride. On May 24, two buses left for Mississippi under heavy guard. As a climax to this ride, the riders were arrested in Jackson, Mississippi, for using terminal facilities. The Freedom Rides continued throughout the summer, ending when the Interstate Commerce Commission issued an order banning segregation of interstate terminal facilities. Following the ICC's ruling, Southern railroads and airlines voluntarily desegregated their facilities.

By 1963 the Civil Rights Movement had reached a new peak of urgency, as thousands of demonstrators poured onto American streets protesting their lack of citizenship. Cities in both the North and South felt the intense push for "freedom now," but nowhere that year was the confrontation between black and white more dramatic than in Birmingham, Alabama.

Birmingham had long been considered the stronghold of Jim Crow. Dr. King had called it "the most thoroughly segregated big city in the U.S."[19] Churches, restaurants, lavatories, drinking fountains, and theaters operated under a system of strict separation of races. Birmingham confined its 100,000 Negroes to cramped ghettos and prevented them from purchasing housing elsewhere. Faced with a 1962 court order to desegregate its parks and playgrounds, the city had closed them to avoid integration. Faced with the Brown decision to desegregate its public schools, the city had ignored the decision. Reporters and writers for major magazines and newspapers had upon occasion drawn poignant comparisons between the racial policies of Birmingham and the practice of "apartheid" in South Africa. Against this city Dr. King opened a six-week campaign to break down the forces of bigotry and oppression.

Project C, as the Birmingham campaign had been designated, started poorly. On April 6, a police blockade halted a demonstration three blocks from its destination at city hall. The marchers refused an order to disband and were arrested. The following day, Palm Sunday, another group of demonstrators

[19]Robert M. Bleiweiss, *Marching to Freedom: The Life of Martin Luther King, Jr.* (American Education Publication, Connecticut, 1968), p. 88.

marched. This time the Birmingham police had enlisted the help of police dogs. Thus, a pattern established itself early. The demonstrators, led by Dr. King, used prayers and songs as their weapons; the police, led by Eugene "Bull" Conner, an outspoken segregationist, used clubs, dogs, and high-powered fire hoses.

On April 12, Dr. King defied a court order banning further demonstrations and was arrested. While in jail he wrote the famous "Letter from a Birmingham Jail" outlining his nonviolent philosophy and carefully explaining how that philosophy might be the last hope for America to avoid "a frightening racial nightmare." A week later he posted bond and returned to his headquarters at a Birmingham motel. Soon after, he made the decision to commit children to the Birmingham struggle.

More than a thousand students answered the call on Thursday, May 2. They marched from the Sixteenth Baptist Church singing "We Shall Overcome," only to be stopped by a wall of police. One thousand people were arrested that day. The next day a larger group marched, and this time Bull Conner ordered fire hoses turned on the demonstrators. Youngsters skidded across the pavement, under cars, and into buildings. The police then waded in with clubs and dogs as the electronic eye of television monitored these scenes for the world. Day after day the demonstrations continued with increasing intensity as an indignant nation watched, urging the federal government to intervene. Finally, President Kennedy sent federal mediators into Birmingham.

After a week of secret negotiations Dr. King and city officials reached an agreement which included the desegregation of public facilities in local stores, equal employment opportunities for blacks, the release of the 2400 Negroes arrested during the demonstration, and the establishment of a biracial committee to look into black-white problems. Segregationists and the local Ku Klux Klan, however, considered the agreement a sellout. On the Saturday following, two dynamite bombs exploded in the home of Dr. King's brother, the Rev. A.D. King, and another at Dr. King's headquarters in the Gaston Motel. Birmingham Negroes were so enraged that the news was followed by several hours of rioting.

The intensity of the Birmingham struggle prompted President Kennedy to adopt a more aggressive civil rights program.

That summer, just a few days after the tragic assassination of the prominent civil rights leader Medgar Evers, Kennedy submitted a civil rights bill to Congress. It called for an end to segregation in places of public accommodation and the empowering of the Attorney General to file suits on behalf of victims of discrimination. It was partly in support of this bill that the Great March on Washington was held in August.

The Great March on Washington, held on August 28, 1963, was the high point of the early Civil Rights Movement. Over 250,000 black and white Americans marched on the nation's capital testifying to the fact that a century after the signing of the Emancipation Proclamation the descendants of the slaves were not yet free. They had journeyed from all parts of the United States to give their support to the concept of a nation where black and white could live together in harmony and equality. In attendance were many prominent civil rights leaders: A. Philip Randolph, who had organized the march; Roy Wilkins of the NAACP; Whitney Young of the National Urban League; John Lewis of SNCC; Dr. Martin Luther King, Jr., of SCLC; and Floyd McKissick of CORE. Although the labor unions did not give their formal support to the march, Walter Reuther also attended.

That afternoon the march proceeded down Constitution and Independence Avenues to the Lincoln Memorial. There the marchers listened to speeches for nearly three hours. After nine speeches, Dr. Martin Luther King, Jr., rose and spoke, expressing the hope and sentiment not only of those present, but of millions of Americans unable to come. Nearing the end of his famous speech, he said:

> I have a dream that one day this nation will rise up and live out the true meaning of its creed: "We hold these truths to be self-evident; that all men are created equal."

> I have a dream that one day on the red hills of Georgia the sons of former slaves and the sons of former slaveowners will be able to sit down together at the table of brotherhood.

> I have a dream that one day even the state of Mississippi, a desert state sweltering with the heat of injustice and oppression, will be transformed into an oasis of freedom and justice.

I have a dream that my four little children will one day live in a nation where they will not be judged by the color of their skin, but by the content of their character.

I have a dream today. . . .

Eighteen days after the March, white reactionaries in Birmingham answered Dr. King's plea for brotherhood. During a Sunday School class a bomb exploded in the Sixteenth Street Baptist Church killing four Negro girls and injuring twenty-one other persons. The nation was once again shocked—but it was a time of shocks. Two months later an assassin killed President Kennedy in Dallas, Texas.

Because of Lyndon Johnson's Southern background, many civil rights leaders feared the loss of executive help they had previously received. Their fears were allayed when the new President pressed for the passage of Kennedy's civil rights bill. Congress, perhaps in tribute to the dead president, acted quickly, and on July 3, 1964, President Johnson signed the Civil Rights Act of 1964 into law.

Once the Civil Rights Act had been passed and accommodation in public facilities had been assured by the federal government, the Civil Rights Movement shifted emphasis from desegregation to the disenfranchisement of the Southern Negro. Since 1961 Robert Moses of SNCC had been conducting voter registration projects in Mississippi. These projects had usually centered around Freedom Schools, which—in addition to teaching basic reading, writing, health care, and Black history—instructed the Mississippi Negro in the complexities of voter registration, Southern-style. Similar projects had been operating in Alabama, but the successes had been unspectacular. Dr. King, realizing that real improvements for the Negro hinged on the power of the ballot box, decided that another Birmingham was needed to dramatize the voting issue. He selected Selma, Alabama.

Selma was often called the "Capital of the Black Belt" and was the seat of Dallas County, where Negro residents were clearly in the majority. Yet, at the beginning of 1965 only 340 of the 15,000 Negroes were registered to vote. Of the 14,000 white population, 9,500 were registered.[20] (In the neighboring

[20]David L. Lewis, *King: A Critical Biography* (New York: Praeger, 1970), pp. 264-266.

counties of Lowndes and Wilcox, where Negroes outnumbered whites four-to-one, not a single Negro was registered.)[21] Dr. King arrived in Selma in January and established campaign headquarters at the Brown Chapel.

As in Birmingham two years earlier, the demonstrations started on a low key. Small groups held daily registration marches to the county courthouse, where they invariably met Sheriff Jim Clark and helmeted deputies. Those refusing to obey Clark's order to disperse were arrested. Soon Selma's jails overflowed and Sheriff Clark had established a reputation equalling that of Bull Conner.

On the first day of February, Dr. King embarked on the second phase of his campaign by leading 260 marchers to the courthouse. He was arrested for "parading without a permit" and remained in jail for nearly a week. While in jail he announced another, more spectacular, demonstration, proposing a march from Selma to the state capitol in Montgomery to petition the state governor for the right to vote.

On Sunday, March 7, 525 marchers carrying bedrolls, knapsacks, and paper bags departed from Brown Chapel for the fifty-mile journey to Montgomery. Despite somewhat inclement weather, and despite a warning from Governor George Wallace that he would not permit the march, the marchers walked two-by-two until they reached Pettus Bridge, which led out of Selma to the state highway. There they met fifty state troopers and a hundred possemen. When the marchers refused to turn around, the troopers and posse attacked using clubs, bullwhips, and teargas until they drove the marchers back to Brown Chapel.

The incident ignited nationwide public anger, and thousands of irate blacks and whites poured into Selma. One of the newly arrived, the Rev. James J. Reed, a white Unitarian minister, was fatally beaten by white hoodlums before a second march could get underway. His death stirred an even greater ferment of public indignation, and President Johnson, in a televised speech, promised a new bill guaranteeing the voting rights of all citizens.

[21]Coretta Scott King, *My Life with Martin Luther King, Jr.* (New York: Avon, 1969), p. 256.

Two weeks after the first aborted march to Montgomery, 3200 black and white marchers again left Selma. This time they received National Guard protection. When they arrived in Montgomery four days later, their numbers had swollen to 25,000. The Selma campaign had been successful. (Later that summer President Johnson signed into law the Voting Rights Act of 1965, which provided for federal registrars to register voters in states refusing to do so.) But even the success of Selma was tainted by violence. Mrs. Viola Liuzzo, a Detroit housewife who had traveled to this Black Belt city with thousands of other angry Americans, was shot to death in her car while helping to return demonstrators to Selma after the Montgomery march.

THE BLACK POWER MOVEMENT

A series of riots erupted in the North during the summer of 1964. In New York City the fatal shooting of James Powell, a Negro student, by police set off riots in Harlem and Brooklyn. Soon Rochester, New York, was in flames, and then Jersey City, New Jersey, Dixmoor, Illinois, and Philadelphia. Like a brutal game of racial dominoes, city after city fell to mob rule. The North, the riots were proving, was not the fabled land of milk and honey after all. Over seven million Negroes were crowded into the slums and ghettos of the major Northern cities, and segregation and discrimination existed as cruelly and efficiently in the North as in any Southern Black Belt county.

Economically, the Northern Negro found himself trapped in an urban jungle of subhuman housing, crime and violence, disease, police harassment, and exploitation by greedy merchants and moneylenders. In the five-year period of severe urban rioting—1964 through 1968—the black worker earned an average of $3,000 less per year than the white worker. Black unemployment remained twice that for whites. Ghetto residents suffered lower life-expectancy and higher infant-mortality rates than the white society. Hospitals, libraries, playgrounds and parks, and other public facilities were lacking in many ghettos, and ill-equipped in others. Schools faced overcrowding, and the facilities and quality of education had fallen so far below that of the white schools that the IQ scores of many black children actually decreased after entering school.[22] To make matters worse, Northern liberals and politicians openly advocated the civil rights cause only so long as it remained in the South. They seemed to consistently overlook the problems in their own backyards. Northern courts and statutes had long offered full equality, but the one thing Northern liberals never seemed to realize was that the realities of forced poverty eluded the rhetoric of constitutional guarantees.

The 1964 and 1965 summer riots—including the explosion in the Watts section of Los Angeles which left thirty-four persons dead and a thousand injured—had a sobering effect upon the Civil Rights Movement. Both the Civil Rights Act of 1964 and the Voting Rights Act of 1965 had been followed by racial violence. The lesson was clear: although the Civil Rights Movement had mobilized the Southern Negro to combat Jim Crow legislation, its successes had left the Northern Negro virtually unaffected. The question remaining was, could the traditional leadership of the Movement help those Negroes whose primary enemy seemed to be poverty and unemployment? Increasingly, the black underclass was turning to the rhetoric of Malcolm X for the answer.

As a minister for the Black Muslims, Malcolm X had preached a doctrine portraying the black race as good and noble and the white race as inherently evil. By the early sixties, he had raised the Muslims to a position of national prominence. Ironically, the fear and hatred White America felt for this man made whites more amenable to the demands of Martin Luther King, Jr., and other moderate leaders. At the same time, black youth and the more radical members of the Civil Rights Movement were turning to Malcolm's philosophy of black pride, black organization, and black determinism as an alternative to non-violence. This conflict resulted in an ideological split within the Civil Rights Movement, which became evident during the summer of 1966.

By 1964 members of SNCC and CORE had grown impatient with the traditional civil rights leadership. They felt it had been

[22]The reader can consult the *Report of the National Advisory Commission on Civil Disorders* (New York: Bantam Books, 1968) for further documentation.

too slow and ineffective, making mere token advances. If any effective changes were to occur, they felt, the changes would have to be the result of more power in the hands of black people. Early in 1966, Stokely Carmichael of SNCC prepared a position paper outlining a philosophy of black power. The paper criticized white participation in the Civil Rights Movement and urged the development of economic and political power bases to effect changes within American society.

Black Power reached national prominence during the June, 1966, Freedom March of James Meredith, whose enrollment four years earlier at the University of Mississippi had resulted in several days of rioting and federal intervention. Meredith, attempting to encourage Negro voting by demonstrating that a Negro could walk safely through the Mississippi of 1966, was shot and wounded by a white sniper. He was rushed to a Memphis hospital where civil rights leaders from across the nation flew to his bedside. It was agreed by these leaders, including Dr. King, who had flown from Chicago, and Stokely Carmichael, then president of SNCC, that Meredith's march would be continued from the spot where he was shot.

In the course of the 200-mile march through Mississippi, the nation was able to see that a major schism had developed in the leadership of the Civil Rights Movement. Dr. King continued to advocate nonviolence and integration, while Stokely Carmichael spoke of black consciousness and physical, economic, and political resistance to white power. At a mass rally in Greenwood, Carmichael electrified the crowd when he said: "The only way we gonna stop them white men from whuppin' us is to take over. We been saying freedom for six years and we ain't got nothin'. What we gonna start saying now is black power." The crowd replied in unison: "Black Power! Black Power! Black Power!"

In many ways the Greenwood crowd chanting "Black Power!" signalled the death of the Civil Rights Movement. Dr. King flew back to Chicago to lead housing marches into the suburb of Cicero, but the influence of nonviolence was never as strong nor as popular as it had been before the Meredith march. Increasingly, the black population and black leaders were turning to the concept of Black Power as a viable way of attaining equality. Many black people continued advocating nonviolence, but for a growing number of blacks it represented a form of submissiveness. Nonviolence, they felt, hinged upon the white establishment's giving equality, and it had been repeatedly demonstrated that the white establishment gave only when forced. Black Power provided a suitable force.

Dr. King continued to be the most influential Negro leader until his assassination, but the years between the Greenwood rally and Dr. King's death were years of turmoil. Rioting in Newark during the summer of 1967 left twenty-three persons dead and precipitated the grim Detroit riot which gave the nation a frightening look at the possibility of civil war between whites and blacks.

The years between Greenwood and Dr. King's death were also years of confusion for the Civil Rights Movement. From demonstrations opposing the Vietnam War to preparations for a "Poor People's Campaign" to eradicate poverty, the Civil Rights Movement seemed to be thrashing about for an issue that would galvanize the impatience of black youth and the growing influence of the Black Power Movement.

On April 4, 1968, an assassin's bullet struck down Dr. Martin Luther King, Jr., in Memphis, Tennessee. He was laid to rest five days later in Atlanta, Georgia. His death sparked a period of rioting across the nation. Beyond that, however, his passing signified the passing of the Civil Rights Movement. In its place came a newer movement, a movement by and for black people. Dr. King had accomplished much in his lifetime. Perhaps his greatest accomplishment was in teaching black people that they could lead themselves. The progression from the Civil Rights Movement to the Black Power Movement was a natural one, for the Civil Rights Movement had prepared the masses for the time when they would no longer need to be led but would determine their own future.

3

VOICES OF CHANGE

THE MARTYRED GIANT: DR. MARTIN LUTHER KING, JR.

MARTIN LUTHER KING, JR., was born in Atlanta, Georgia, on January 15, 1929. His father was pastor of Ebenezer Baptist Church, a member of the NAACP, and a prominent leader of anti-segregation forces in Atlanta. This undoubtedly provided a strong impetus for the boy who would one day receive the Nobel Peace Prize for his efforts in combatting racial inequality. At the age of nineteen King graduated from Morehouse College, and three years later he received his Bachelor of Divinity degree from Crozer Theological Seiminary. At Crozer he became interested in the life and philosophy of Mahatma Gandhi after hearing a sermon on Gandhi's use of love as a force for good. From this, the idea of nonviolent resistance to racial discrimination and segregation was born.

King met Coretta Scott while he was attending Boston University. She was a graduate student at the New England Conservatory of Music studying to be a concert singer. They were married on June 18, 1953. In 1955, King received his Ph.D. in theology and became resident pastor of the Dexter Avenue Baptist Church in Montgomery, Alabama.

When Mrs. Rosa Parks of Montgomery refused to give up her bus seat to a white passenger on December 1, 1955, Dr. King rose to the forefront of national attention by successfully leading the Montgomery Bus Boycott. For the first time he was able to put into large-scale practice his principle of nonviolent resistance. One year and two months later he formed the Southern Christian Leadership Conference to combat racial segregation in the South.

During the early sixties, Dr. King led and promoted civil rights demonstrations throughout the South. From Selma to Birmingham, he and his followers challenged segregation of public facilities and encouraged voter-registration drives. In 1964, at the age of thirty-five, he was awarded the Nobel Peace Prize. In the latter half of the sixties, he increasingly concentrated his attention on problems in the Northern states. He attacked inadequate housing, poor educational facilities, and *de facto* segregation by leading massive marches and bartering with city officials to promote total equality for Black Americans.

In 1968, to illustrate the plight of the nation's poor, he organized the Poor People's Campaign to be held that August in Washington, D.C. Before the campaign, however, he went to Memphis to participate in a demonstration of striking sanitation workers. While standing on the balcony of the Lorraine Motel, on April 4, 1968, Dr. King was shot by an assassin.

After his death, the Civil Rights Movement assumed a new militancy, becoming for all purposes a Black Power Movement. Leaders rose and fell, but no leader reached the status of the "martyred giant."

BIG RED: MALCOLM X

Malcolm Little was born to Louise and the Reverend Earl Little on May 19, 1925, in Omaha, Nebraska. Soon after, his family moved to Lansing, Michigan, where his father was an outspoken proponent of Marcus Garvey's "Back to Africa" movement. When Malcolm was six, his father was mysteriously killed in downtown Lansing. His mother Louise tried to keep her family of eight children together for six years before suffering a nervous breakdown. She was committed to the state hospital at Kalamazoo, and her children were distributed to various relatives and foster homes. Malcolm was sent to live with a foster family in Mason, Michigan. In 1940, however, he caught a Greyhound bus and went to live with his half-sister in

Boston. One year later, at the age of seventeen, he moved to Harlem, where he built a reputation as a hustler.

Malcolm Little was known to other Harlem hustlers as "Detroit Red," and developed expertise in narcotics, prostitution, gambling, and larceny. At the age of twenty, he organized a burglary ring that operated in the Boston area. In 1946 he was arrested and convicted on a burglary charge and sentenced to ten years in Charlestown State Prison. After being transferred to Concord Prison in 1948, he received a letter from his brother telling about the Nation of Islam. Malcolm began corresponding with Elijah Muhammad, and after his release in 1952, Malcolm Little hurried to Detroit and formally joined the Black Muslims.

Malcolm X possessed a natural organizational ability. He was a dynamic speaker, and from his studies in prison an educated man. He rose quickly in the Muslim religion to become Elijah Muhammad's number-one minister. New chapters mushroomed across the country as Malcolm X carried the "message of Allah" from city to city. As new mosques grew from his indefatigable energy, so did his reputation as a fiery orator. Black audiences loved his fierce diatribes against the "blue-eyed devils," while White America experienced fear and revulsion. In 1963 Malcolm had a disagreement with Elijah Muhammad and was censured as a spokesman for the Black Muslims. The same year, he completed his *Hajj,* the pilgrimage to Mecca.

Malcolm X had always believed that racism was an inherent affliction within the human race. In Mecca he saw for the first time in his life the total absence of racism. All men of all colors were equal. From this, and from his subsequent journey through Africa, he learned that a world could exist free of all prejudice.

When Malcolm returned to the United States, he formed the Organization of Afro-American Unity, an amalgamation of black organizations fighting white racism. In 1965 he dictated his autobiography to Alex Haley and prophesied that he would never live to see it published. His prophecy came true. On February 21, 1965, at approximately 3:30 p.m., Malcolm X died from gunshot wounds received while he was speaking at the Audubon Ballroom in Harlem.

STOKELY

Stokely Carmichael was born in Port-of-Spain, Trinidad, on June 21, 1941. He lived the first ten years of his life in comparative freedom from racial discrimination. This idyllic life was shattered, however, when his family moved to Harlem in 1952. In the young Carmichael's eyes, the poverty and squalor greeting him in Harlem was appalling. He experienced firsthand the manner in which the white power structure suppressed and destroyed the spirit of the black man. He joined the Civil Rights Movement while still in his teens and—after graduating from Howard University in 1964 with a degree in philosophy—rose to a position of leadership in SNCC. In 1965 he wrote a position paper denouncing white participation in the civil rights struggle. The paper argued that white involvement in SNCC was a basic handicap, watering down any concerted black action. SNCC as an organization should be all black. The paper further suggested that the United Nations be petitioned to designate black people in America as "exploited colonials," thus making racism an international issue with international implications.[23]

In May of 1967, Carmichael resigned from SNCC. He traveled for a few months, visiting communist and free-world nations. Soon after his return to the United States, he married the entertainer Miriam Makeba and retired into relative seclusion from public view.

ELDRIDGE CLEAVER

Eldridge Cleaver was born in Wabbaseka, Arkansas, in 1935. From there his family moved to Phoenix and then to Los Angeles. His early life fit into the pattern of the hard-core ghetto experience, where prostitution, drug addiction, murder, rape, and other harsh realities are commonplace. By the time he reached junior high school, he was arrested for petty theft and sent to the Fred C. Nelles School for Boys. After his release, he entered Belmont High School in South Pasadena. In 1953 he made a position on the football team, but he was unable to play in regular season because of his subsequent arrest for selling

[23]Lerone Bennett, Jr., "Stokely Carmichael: Architect of Black Power," *Ebony* (September, 1966), pp. 25-32.

marijuana. Cleaver finished high school in Soledad Prison and was paroled at the age of twenty-one. Eleven months later he was arrested for rape and convicted of assault-with-intent-to-kill. He was sentenced to two-to-fourteen in Folsom Prison. While serving his term, he came under the influence of the Black Muslims. The teachings of the Nation of Islam, especially Malcolm X, inspired him. He had been a voracious reader at Soledad, and at Folsom his reading intensified. Soon he began writing and publishing articles in *Ramparts Magazine.* He was released in December of 1966 and met with the editors of *Ramparts,* who helped him edit his articles into the book *Soul on Ice.*

Cleaver joined the staff of *Ramparts* in 1967. A short time later, he met and married Kathleen Neal, a diplomat's daughter and member of SNCC. The same year, he met Huey P. Newton and joined the Black Panther Party, serving as Minister of Information. When the Panthers aligned themselves with the Peace and Freedom Party prior to the 1968 presidential election, Cleaver won the presidential nomination over Dick Gregory. Meanwhile, his parole board viewed his political activities with disapproval. They regarded this activity and his alleged involvement in a shoot-out which left Black Panther Bobby Hutton dead as a clear violation of his parole terms. Sometime in November, Cleaver disappeared. He later turned up in Algeria, where he continued to be a militant voice for black nationalism.

4
VIOLENCE IN THE CITIES

AT 7:00 P.M., AUGUST 11, 1965, a white motorcycle patrolman stopped a car driven by twenty-one-year-old Marquette Frye at the corner of 116th and Avalon, near the Watts section of Los Angeles. Frye was arrested for drunken driving. Frye's passenger, his older brother Ronald, asked and was refused permission to drive his brother's car home. Ronald then walked the two blocks to his home to get his mother and at approximately 7:15 returned to the scene with Mrs. Frye. At the same time, a second motorcycle patrolman, a patrol car, and a tow truck arrived. As officers tried to place the arrested Marquette into the patrol car, a scuffle broke out, and during the struggle officers knocked Mrs. Frye out of the way and struck Marquette on the forehead with a nightstick. By this time the crowd of spectators numbered about 300. They grew hostile. Three more highway patrolmen arrived in response to a police call for assistance. The trio—Marquette, Ronald, and Mrs. Frye—were subdued, and as the officers prepared to leave someone in the crowd spat on one of the patrolmen. Two officers pushed into the crowd and arrested a young Negro woman and a man. At 7:40 p.m., all officers withdrew, the last patrol car being stoned. Rumors about the arrest spread and small groups of angry Negroes began roaming along Avalon Boulevard. Automobiles entering the area were stoned and motorists pulled from their cars and beaten. A meeting the following day failed to quiet the tension and violence. Looting, arson, rock-throwing, and other violence escalated on a large scale, with cries of "Burn, baby, burn."

The Watts riot of 1965, which lasted six days—from Wednesday, August 11, to Tuesday, August 17—shocked the nation. In 1964 the Urban League had rated Los Angeles first among sixty-eight cities examined for opportunities for Negroes. When the Watts riot erupted, it pointed out just how dismal life had become for the urban Negro. The riot area covered nearly fifty square miles, and nearly a thousand buildings were looted, damaged, or destroyed. The California National Guard had to be called in, but by the time they were able to restore order, thirty-four persons had been killed and 1,032 injured. Property damage soared to $35 or $40 million.

THE REPORT BY THE GOVERNOR'S COMMISSION ON THE LOS ANGELES RIOT

After the last fires had been doused and order had been restored to the Watts section of Los Angeles, the governor of California commissioned a study into the causes of the riot. John McCone, former head of the Central Intelligence Agency, headed the group, and after a hundred days of hearings and deliberations issued a report entitled *Violence in the City—An End or a Beginning.* In summing up, the commission stated in its report: "The study of the Los Angeles riots which we have now completed brought us face to face with the deepening problems that confront America." The report said that they were "the problems of transition created by three decades of change" in which patterns of urban and rural life had been drastically altered.

During World War II there had been a great migration to the Northern cities by Southern Negroes. At first the problems associated with this migration were not readily apparent "because job opportunities existed in the war plants located in our cities." But the problems facing the transplanted Negro were soon manifested as wartime jobs disappeared and industry turned increasingly to mechanization. "Hence, equality of opportunity, a privilege he sought and expected," the report said of the Southern Negro, "proved more of an illusion than a fact. The Negro found that he entered the competitive life of the city with very real handicaps: he lacked education, training, and experience, and his handicaps were aggravated by racial barriers which were more traditional than legal." The report explained that the Negro then found himself "in a situation in which providing a livelihood for himself and his family was most difficult and at times desperate." The report maintained that "with the passage of time, altogether too often the rural Negro who has come to the city sinks into despair." The second and third generations then "inherit this feeling but seek release, not in apathy, but in ways which, if allowed to run unchecked, offer nothing but tragedy to America."

In its conclusion the report made a number of recommendations, including the "establishment of a special school program, creation of training courses, and correction of misunderstandings involving law enforcement." The commission made these recommendations because, as the members said, "we are convinced the Negro can no longer exist, as he has, with the disadvantages which separate him from the rest of society, deprive him of employment, and cause him to drift aimlessly through life."

DETROIT

At 3:45 a.m., Sunday, July 23, 1967, the Detroit Police Department's vice-squad raided a "blind pig" at the corner of 12th Street and Clairmount. Inside they found a party for several servicemen, two of whom were recently back from Vietnam. All eighty-two patrons of the establishment were arrested, and in the hour it took to remove them from the building a crowd of approximately 200 bystanders gathered. The weather was warm and humid. Almost immediately, rumors began circulating that the police had used excessive force during the raid. The number of persons along 12th Street increased and window smashing and looting began. By 7:50 a.m., when a police commando unit attempted to clear the area, the number had swollen to an estimated 3,000 people. Violence steadily increased throughout the day.

The Detroit race riot lasted four days, from Sunday to Thursday, dwarfing the city's infamous race riot of 1943, when thirty-four persons had been killed and $2 million in property destroyed. During the course of the 1967 riot, 8,000 Michigan National Guardsmen and 4,700 federal troops were deployed to the Detroit riot area, augmenting the Detroit Police Department and the Michigan State Police. Looting, arson, scattered incidents of sniping—and troop inexperience—characterized this riot, which left forty-three persons dead and property damage set at somewhere between $22 and $40 million.

THE REPORT OF THE NATIONAL ADVISORY COMMISSION ON CIVIL DISORDERS

Two days after the 1967 Detroit riot, President Johnson appointed the Commission on Civil Disorders to investigate the causes of racial violence which had plagued America for three years and had reached a frightening intensity during the summer of 1967. The commission was headed by Governor Otto Kerner of Illinois and early in 1968 reported its findings. The basic conclusion of the study group was a frightening one, stating that: "Our nation is moving toward two societies, one black, one white—separate and unequal." In dealing with the basic causes of the riots, the report—as had the McCone report following the Watts riot—placed much of the blame on historical developments within the United States. "The record before this Commission," the report stated, "reveals that the causes of recent racial disorders are embedded in a massive tangle of issues and circumstances—social, economic, political, and psychological—which arise out of the historic pattern of Negro-white relations in America."

The Kerner Commission first took a look at the broad implications of these historical developments, striking hard at the racial attitude and behavior of White America. "Race prejudice has shaped our history decisively in the past . . . " the report said, and then it carried this supposition to its logical conclusion: "White racism is essentially responsible for the explosive mixture which has been accumulating in our cities since the end of World War II." White racial attitudes, the report continued, have yielded three "bitter fruits." The first of these fruits "is surely the continuing exclusion of great numbers of Negroes from the benefits of economic progress through discrimination in employment and education, and their enforced confinement in segregated housing and schools." The second of these fruits "is the massive and growing concentration of impoverished Negroes in our major cities resulting from Negro migration from the rural South, rapid population growth and the continuing movement of the white middle class to the suburbs." Third, "segregation and poverty have intersected to destroy opportunity and hope and to enforce failure."

"The ghettos," the report said, "too often mean men and women without jobs, families without men, and schools where children are processed instead of educated, until they return to the street—to crime, to narcotics, to dependency on welfare, and to bitterness and resentment against society in general and white society in particular." And as the ghettos deteriorate, the report explained, the white and black middle class "have prospered to a degree unparalleled in the history of civilization." This has added to the bitterness of the ghetto resident, for "Through television—the universal appliance in the ghetto—and the other media of mass communications, this affluence has been endlessly flaunted before the eyes of the Negro poor and the jobless ghetto youth."

Black Americans have aspirations as Americans. "They seek to share in both the material resources of our system and its intangible benefits—dignity, respect, and acceptance." Yet, within the ghetto "it is rare that either aspiration is achieved." Thus, frustration, bitterness, and resentment against white society have created an emotional climate ripe for violence among ghetto blacks. To this mixture, the report says, were added three ingredients which acted as catalysts.

The first catalyst was the growing awareness by Northern Negroes of the gap between promise and fulfillment. The report says that the "victories of the civil rights movement have led to frustration, hostility and cynicism," because the "dramatic struggle for equal rights in the South has sensitized Northern Negroes to the economic inequalities reflected in the deprivations of ghetto life."

Second, the report cites the legitimation of violence in American society. "A climate that tends toward the approval and encouragement of violence as a form of protest," the report says, has been created by white terrorism directed against nonviolent protest, including instances of abuse and even murder of some civil rights workers in the South. . . ." This has tended to remove the restraints against violence, a condition "reinforced by a general erosion of respect for authority in American society. . . ."

"Finally," the report continues, "many Negroes have come to believe that they are being exploited politically and economically by the white 'power structure.'" They have been overwhelmed by a feeling of powerlessness, the report explains, because they lacked "the channels of communication, influence and appeal that traditionally have been available to ethnic minorities within the city" to enable them to escape the ghettos. This has "led some to the conviction that there is no effective alternative to violence as a means of expression and redress, as a way of 'moving the system.'" This, in turn, has produced an "alienation and hostility toward the institutions of law and government and the white society which controls them."

"These conditions," the report explains, "have created a volatile mixture of attitudes and beliefs which needs only a spark to ignite mass violence." Invariably, that spark is supplied by the police. "Harlem, Watts, Newark and Detroit were precipitated by arrests of Negroes by white policemen for minor offenses." The report maintains that the police "are inevitably involved in sharper and more frequent conflicts with ghetto residents than with the residents of other areas." Thus, "police have come to symbolize white power, white racism, and white repression." And it was a mixture of many things, the report says, ignited by an incident of a police arrest, which set off the mighty Detroit riot of 1967.

5

FORCES OF CHANGE

THE BLACK MUSLIMS

DURING THE SUMMER OF 1930, W.D. Fard, a peddler of silks, yard goods, and African artifacts, mysteriously appeared in the ghetto of Detroit, Michigan. The enigmatic figure sold his wares door to door and at the same time told his customers about a religion practiced by black men in Asia and Africa. Four years later, around June of 1934, he disappeared, leaving behind the Nation of Islam, led by a close disciple called Elijah Muhammad, formerly Elijah Poole of Sandersville, Georgia. An offshoot of the Moslem religion, the Black Muslims became a new voice in the ghetto and espoused black supremacy, separatism, and racial pride.

The Black Muslims, with an estimated following of 100,000, maintain a strict code of social and moral discipline. Members must be employed and are forbidden to smoke, drink, take narcotics, dance, gamble, commit adultery, or engage in any activity damaging to physical and spiritual well-being. Muslim doctrine professes racial superiority and has prophesied a day of Armageddon when the white race will be destroyed by Allah.

The eventual aim of the Black Muslims—like that of the Republic of New Africa and other separatist groups—is to establish a Black Nation for the descendants of American slaves. Presently, however, they resemble a "nation within a nation." They operate their own schools, farms, restaurants, bakeries, dry cleaners, and barber shops and approach the status of an independent, self-supporting community in the cities where they have their mosques. They have their own newspaper, *Muhammad Speaks,* and their own police force, the *Fruit of Islam.* They actively recruit within the ghettos and—although their membership remains small—their ideas, especially regarding Black Pride and Black Capitalism, have spread.

The Muslims gained national prominence during the midfifties, when Malcolm X launched his fierce diatribes against white oppression. Mainly through his efforts, the Black Muslims gained popularity among Afro-Americans and grew to include mosques in nearly every major city. As Malcolm X organized the religious growth of the Nation of Islam, Muhammad Ali—the former Cassius Clay and world heavyweight boxing champion—pressed the question of its legitimacy. Ali sought exemption from the military draft on the ground that he was a Black Muslim minister, thus winning recognition for the Nation of Islam as a legal organized religion within the United States.

THE BLACK PANTHERS

Partly as a result of conditions in the Los Angeles ghetto of Watts, and partly as a result of instances of police brutality and negligence in the ghettos across the nation, Bobby Seale and Huey P. Newton formed the Black Panther Party for Self-defense in the spring of 1966. Two former students from Merritt College, Seale and Newton organized the Panthers around ten basic points:

1. The power for black people to determine the destiny of the black community;
2. Full employment for all blacks in the United States;
3. Adequate, sanitary shelter for black people;
4. All black men to be exempt from military service;
5. A decent, relevant education for black children;
6. An end to white racist businessmen exploiting black people in their own community;
7. An end to police brutality in the ghetto;
8. Black prisoners to be released from all penal institutions and to be retried by a jury of their peers;
9. All future black people charged of crimes to be tried in

a court and by a jury of their peer group (the peer
group consisting of other black people from the same
community and socio-economic background); and
10. A nation and world living at peace and equality with
itself.[24]

During the late sixties and early seventies, the Panthers were
a politically-oriented revolutionary group whose ideology was
based upon the teachings and writings of Mao, Frantz Fanon
(*The Wretched of the Earth*), and Carlos Marighella (*Mini-
manual of the Urban Guerrilla*). Their aim was to change existing conditions within the United States. They saw the instrument of change as being violence, because they felt that all
other methods had failed to bring about equality, brotherhood,
and freedom for all men. They professed to want an open
society established upon the principles of humanitarianism and
community rule and vigorously maintained that they were not
anti-white, but anti-injustice. They felt that when a system
infringes upon the physical and human rights of any group, that
system must be destroyed.

Aside from the more sensational elements of the Black
Panther Party, they performed valuable services for the black
community. They operated massive breakfast programs for
ghetto youth; they maintained day-care centers to allow ghetto
mothers to work; they provided legal counseling for black
people; and in a few cases they furnished community control
when the existing governmental agencies failed to act.

THE CONGRESS OF RACIAL EQUALITY

The Congress of Racial Equality (CORE), which staged the
famous "Freedom Rides" of 1961, was formed in 1942 by
James Farmer to combat segregation and weaknesses in the legal
system. A pioneer in the techniques of nonviolent resistance,
including the sit-in, CORE worked closely with SNCC and
SCLC in the desegregation of public facilities during the late
fifties and early sixties. While helping improve the Negro's
plight through the encouragement of self-help programs, CORE,

[24]Ten points taken from Gene Marine, *The Black Panthers* (New York:
Signet, 1969).

like the NAACP, actively worked for racial equality in the United States.

THE NATIONAL ASSOCIATION FOR THE ADVANCEMENT OF COLORED PEOPLE

Originally organized in 1910 as a reaction against the rash of lynchings in both the North and South, the NAACP is the most powerful of civil rights organizations. It has an integrated membership of approximately 500,000 socially aware individuals dedicated to the betterment of the condition of Negroes in America. Its battleground is the courtroom, where it works to abolish all forced segregation, to insure equal educational opportunities for black children, to guarantee voting rights for the Negro, and to secure enforcement of civil rights legislation. One of its most important cases was *Brown v. Board of Education,* when on May 17, 1954, the Supreme Court ruled that segregation of public schools on the basis of race was unconstitutional.

THE NATIONAL URBAN LEAGUE

The National Urban League was founded in 1910 to assist the urban adjustment of Negroes migrating from the South. An interracial organization, the League has aided the black community with a variety of social services, but its primary task has been to find jobs for Negroes. As such, it acts as a liaison between industry and the ghetto. The Urban League has largely become an employment center and, ironically, has opened more job opportunities than there have been qualified Negroes to fill. Presently the League is working for more training programs to correct this situation.

THE STUDENT NON-VIOLENT COORDINATING COMMITTEE

In April of 1960, James Foreman and Martin Luther King, Jr., established SNCC to organize the sit-ins in the South. SNCC revitalized the Civil Rights Movement by using college students and young people to confront the forces of discrimination. It had an "electric" quality that attracted thousands of supporters. Volunteers clad in denims and straw hats swallowed abuse and risked their lives to live among Southern Negroes to help them unite against the white power structure. In 1966 the organization changed when Stokely Carmichael drew up his position paper calling for the exclusion of white members and the adoption of a policy of Black Power. At that point SNCC became a militant voice of Black Nationalism.

THE SOUTHERN CHRISTIAN LEADERSHIP CONFERENCE

The Southern Christian Leadership Conference, founded by Martin Luther King, Jr., in 1957, is an organization believing that religion and the church should be the main force in the struggle for equality. SCLC favored the principles of nonviolent protest based on the teachings of Gandhi.

During the sixties, SCLC and CORE organized "freedom rides" and sit-ins throughout the South, bringing an end to segregated bus lines and public facilities. Dr. King then turned his attention to the North and held massive voter-registration campaigns in cities like Chicago.

The highlight of SCLC was the Great March on Washington on August 28, 1963, when nearly a quarter of a million black and white Americans protested the oppression of Negroes in the United States.

SCLC changed hands in April, 1968, when Dr. King was assassinated. Since that time, the strength of the organization has continually declined.

PART TWO

BROWN POWER:

THE MEXICAN AMERICANS

6

BROWN POWER

LA RAZA IN REVOLT

IN THE VINEYARDS of California's fertile San Joaquin Valley groups of striking farm workers waved the new symbol of Mexican American pride, the red flag with the black Aztec eagle, and shouted, *"Huelga! Huelga! Huelga!"* (Strike! Strike! Strike!). Cesar Chavez and his National Farm Workers Association had already signed contracts with the major wine producers, but other large growers had held out. In a move which involved the entire nation in the plight of the farm worker, Chavez issued a plea for the boycott of table grapes not bearing the union insignia.

In Los Angeles, the chairman of the Mayor's Youth Advisory Council, David Sanchez, himself having experienced police brutality, formed the militant Brown Berets for the self-defense of Mexican Americans.

On June 5, 1967, a band of armed men descended upon the courthouse in the village of Tierra Amarilla, New Mexico. They had come to arrest the District Attorney of Santa Fe, Rio Arriba, and Los Alamos counties for his reported harassment of members of the *Alianza Federal de Mercedes* (Federal Alliance of Land Grants). The raid on the Tierra Amarilla courthouse left a state policeman and a deputy sheriff wounded, and scores of militia, including an armored tank, scoured the nearby hills for Reies Lopez Tijerina, the fiery leader of the land-grant movement.

In Crystal City, Texas, the Spinach Capital of America, the youthful founder of the Mexican American Youth Organization, MAYO, returned from St. Mary's University in San Antonio with a master's degree in political science. José Angel Gutierrez formed an independent political party, *La Raza Unida,* and shattered the established order of Anglo control.

In Denver the spunky ex-prizefighter Rodolfo "Corky" Gonzales formed the Crusade for Justice and established the "Spiritual Plan of Aztlan," calling for, among other things, an appeal to the United Nations for a plebiscite to be held in the Southwest.

In the *barrios* (Mexican American districts) of Los Angeles, San Antonio, Denver, and Chicago, thousands of Mexican American students staged walkouts protesting racist teachers, the omission from school curriculums of studies in Mexican and Mexican American history and culture, and the prohibition of Spanish on school grounds. The decade of the sixties, it seemed, was feeling the rumblings of what Walt Whitman had termed the "sleeping giant," the 7.5 million Mexican Americans in the United States.

Much of the thrust for this power movement came from younger Mexican Americans (*chicanos**** as they fondly call themselves). Having been educated in American schools, these young activists were sufficiently "Americanized" to demand their rights as U.S. citizens. They were often militant and outspoken, reflecting a growing sense of urgency among Mexican Americans.

At present Mexican Americans constitute the second largest minority group. The majority live in the five Southwestern states—California, Arizona, New Mexico, Colorado, and Texas. On the whole, Mexican Americans are poor, under-educated, and politically impotent. They have traditionally occupied the rung on the social and economic ladder just above the American Indian; but the sixties saw that begin to change. Nationalism crept through the urban *barrios,* stirring the descendants of the Aztecs to cultural pride and a sense of unity. The Mexican Americans, *La Santa Raza* (the holy race), began asserting

---

*Probably a shortened form of *mexicano(s),* with the first syllable dropped and the *x* pronounced *ch,* as by Mexico's Chihuahua Indians.

themselves in a movement to improve their social and economic condition while preserving their cultural heritage.

Student organizations, underground newspapers, and confrontations with the "establishment" sprang up across the United States, forewarning of a second major civil rights movement. Phrases like "the Bronze People," "Brown Is Beautiful," and "Viva La Raza" became the cultural slogans of older and younger Chicanos alike, and cultural nationalism became a dominant theme. Revolutionary heroes like Emiliano Zapata, Pancho Villa, and the first Indian president of Mexico, Benito Juarez, were resurrected from the Mexican past to serve as models for the advocates of Chicano Power; and on the walls, doors, and even ceilings of Chicano headquarters the proclamation "Viva La Revolucion" reminded leaders of the 1910 Mexican Revolution which changed the course of Mexican history, making that nation more responsive to the needs of the people. Chicano Power, Brown Power, became a cry bursting upon the United States, demanding cultural autonomy and opportunity from the land of opportunity.

THE GROWTH OF A MOVEMENT

For more than a generation forces have been at work shaping the infant Chicano Power movement. Significant numbers of soldiers returning from the battlefields of World War II went on to college via the GI Bill of Rights. Instead of passing into the Anglo society, many of these young veterans returned to the urban *barrios* intent upon making conditions better for the Chicano. As Dr. Julian Nava, noted writer and historian, commented: "My generation, the Chicano veterans of World War II, fought to have our people called *Mexican American;* and many of us suffered. We lost our jobs and were forced to leave our homes. We were jailed, beaten, and even killed."[1] The bulk of these returning veterans formed or joined organizations designed to apply pressure through legal channels. Meanwhile, other leaders labored to open doors too long closed to Mexican Americans.

[1]Excerpt from a speech delivered at O'Rafferty High School, Lansing, Michigan, August 7, 1971.

In California, Cesar Chavez left Saul Alinsky's Community Action Organization and, armed with the belief that concerted action is the only way the poor can gain political and economic power, moved his family to Delano in order to organize a farm workers' union. Laboring sixteen hours a day, Chavez succeeded in building a union, and, perhaps more importantly, succeeded in forging a national identity for the Chicano. Cesar Chavez became a symbol of Mexican American pride and aspirations. In New Mexico, Reies Lopez Tijerina returned from Spain after an exhaustive study of Spanish land grants. Working for the restoration of land guaranteed the defeated Mexicans after the Mexican-American War, he evoked widespread sympathy from Chicanos and Anglos alike. Although no land was restored, nor indemnities paid, he restored a vital element to many Chicanos—pride in the Mexican American heritage. And in Denver, "Corky" Gonzales left the boxing ring and formed the Crusade for Justice. Calling for a new nation, Aztlan, Gonzales reached deeply into Mexican American pride. His epic poem "I Am Joaquín" was immediately embraced as the cry of the contemporary Chicano. An excerpt reads:

> *I am Joaquín*
> *Lost in a world of confusion,*
> *Caught up in a whirl of*
> *   Anglo society,*
> *Confused by the rules,*
> *Scorned by the attitudes,*
> *Suppressed by the manipulations,*
> *And destroyed*
> *   by modern life.* [2]

The growing militancy of the Chicano Power Movement received a good deal of impetus from the Civil Rights Movement. The Chicanos were quick to see that the Anglo society responded to Black Power tactics and that in an America growing increasingly "poverty-conscious" the majority of the rewards from such activity was going to the blacks. Adopting tactics of black activists, Chicanos began applying them for their own needs. Confrontation became increasingly acceptable among the members of La Raza. Boycotts, sit-ins, school walk-

[2]Rodolfo Gonzales, "I Am Joaquín." Copy supplied by the Crusade for Justice, 1567 Downing, Denver, Colorado.

outs, marches, power-bloc and swing voting, community activism in local issues, and even violence began yielding results. And for the more conservative members of the *barrios*, the passage by Congress of the Economic Opportunity Act had a profound impact. The War on Poverty taught the Mexican Americans techniques of community action, and it also raised the expectations of the Chicano poor.[3] With urban renewal crashing through large urban *barrios*, destroying the social isolation which had buffered the Mexican American against his social and economic condition, more and more Chicanos began showing a willingness to use confrontation.

The major aims of the Chicano Power Movement have been (1) to improve the economic, social, and political condition of Mexican Americans and enable them to establish political, social, and economic hegemony over their communities; (2) to instill cultural pride in Mexican Americans; and (3) to bring about a greater recognition from the Anglo society of the Mexican American culture, language, and traditions. By 1972, however, it found itself in a curious limbo.

Moderates valued assimilation into the Anglo society through legal and nonviolent channels, while many extremists talked of violent confrontation to force the society to respond. Still others demanded a total rejection of the Anglo society, choosing instead cultural and social isolation. In whatever form, though, Chicano Power stressed education as an absolute necessity for self-determination. As one *barrio* leader said, "Education is our primary goal. With proper psychological and educational tools, the rest will come." Running a close second, and to many a strong first, was the political arena. Martin Moralez, a militant leader in Michigan, commented, "Politics is the game. The others [leaders] stress economics, education, and marches, but politics is where the action is. You have to beat the Anglo at his own thing—politics. You have to outsmart him using his rules to get what you want."

EDUCATION: A PRIORITY GOAL

In March, 1968, 15,000 Chicano students walked out of five Los Angeles high schools. Within hours of the "blowout"—as

[3]"Chicanos Campaign for a Better Deal," *Business Week* (May 29, 1971), p. 48.

the students called their strike—the entire East Los Angeles *barrio* had unified behind the strikers. The demands presented to the Board of Education called for revisions in textbooks and curriculum so as to include Mexican American contributions to the history of the United States, the transfer of racist teachers, the training of school personnel in Spanish language and culture, and additional Spanish-language library materials. The school board reacted quickly by dismissing Sal Castro from its teaching staff for his part in the "conspiracy." When news of the suspension reached the Mexican American community, parents and students jammed the Board of Education's offices and staged a week-long sit-in until the school board relented, reversing its suspension order. The Mexican Americans had won an important victory. The blowouts welded student activists and traditional adult conservatives into a significant power unit capable of challenging the educational system and forcing long-needed reforms.

The Chicano Power Movement sees the educational system as its primary target, for education has been a dismal chapter in the Mexican American past. Mexican Americans average four years less schooling than Anglos, and two years less than blacks. Almost half of the Spanish-speaking residents of the five Southwestern states have fewer than five years of schooling, and the worst dropout rates come from schools with a predominance of Mexican American students. At the heart of this record of underachievement lies the fact that schools have ignored the language and culture of their Mexican American students.

In the past few years, several organizations have sprung up to improve the education of Mexican American youngsters. Among the more vocal are groups like the Association of Mexican American Educators, the United Mexican American Students, and the Mexican American Students Association, who wage a continual war demanding the recognition of the Mexican American cultural heritage and the establishment of bilingual schools where English is taught as a second language. "The schools have failed us," said one student interviewed, "and we intend to correct that." In the words of another Chicano, a female graduate of an East Los Angeles high school interviewed by the Sillas Committee:

From the time we first begin attending school, we hear about how great and wonderful our United States is, about our democratic American heritage, but little about our splendid and magnificent Mexican heritage and culture. What little we do learn about Mexicans is how they mercilessly slaughtered the brave Texans at the Alamo, but we never hear about the child heroes of Mexico who courageously threw themselves from the heights of Chapultepec rather than allow themselves and their flag to be captured by the attacking Americans.

We look for others like ourselves in these history books, for something to be proud of for being a Mexican, and all we see in books, magazines, films, and TV shows are stereotypes of a dark, dirty, smelly man with a tequila bottle in one hand, a dripping taco in the other, a serape wrapped around him, and a big sombrero.

But we are not the dirty, stinking winos that the Anglo world would like to point out as Mexican. We begin to think that maybe the Anglo teacher is right, that maybe we are inferior, that we do not belong in this world, that—as some teachers actually tell students to their faces—we should go back to Mexico and quit causing problems for America.[4]

THE POLITICS OF POWER

The statue of Popeye holding a can of spinach symbolizes Crystal City, a quiet farmtown in southwest Texas. Much of the community's economic life is tied to the spinach industry, a fact reflected by the population. Fully 85 percent of the 10,000 residents are Mexican American farm workers, while the remaining 15 percent are Anglos who control 95 percent of the farms and businesses.[5]

For generations, the decision-making institutions have responded to Anglo control—a case of minority rule which tends to be the norm rather than the exception in southwest

[4]John H. Burma, ed., *Mexican-Americans in the United States* (Cambridge, Mass.: Schenkman, 1970), p. 291, citing an article by Charles A. Ericksen, "Uprising in the Barrios," *American Education* (November, 1968).

[5]Antonio Camejo cites these statistics in an expanded introduction for the pamphlet *La Raza Unida Party in Texas* (New York: Pathfinder Press, 1970), p. 3. A shorter version appeared in *The Militant* (June 19, 1970).

Texas. In 1963, however, Crystal City's Mexican American population decided to challenge the existing political order. They elected a Chicano mayor, but the Anglo power structure quickly reduced him to a mere figurehead. Noting the stirrings of militancy in the Mexican American community, Crystal City's Anglos embarked upon a somewhat different political course. Instead of backing local Anglo politicians, they threw their support behind Mexican American *vendidos* (sell-outs) and *Tio Tacos* (Uncle Toms). For the six years following the 1963 election the Anglos managed to maintain control. Then, in the spring of 1969, the symbol of Crystal City took on a new look.

During a Chicano student boycott, a group of students painted Popeye brown. The stirrings of militancy were peaking, and even the economic, legal, and political resources of the Anglos could not check the burgeoning movement. Crystal City's Mexican American population was united behind a new independent Chicano party, *La Raza Unida Party*. In the year following they would wrest control of the political power structure from Anglo hands. Electing a Chicano majority to the school board, they would ban culturally biased IQ tests and institute bilingual education in grades K through 3, a culturally relevant curriculum, and a free breakfast and lunch program. Attacking the city council, they would force other reforms: the jurisdiction of the state police and Texas Rangers in Crystal City would be revoked, their function being replaced by an all-Chicano police force; a municipal tax exemption for the Del Monte Corporation would be repealed; and the Chicanos would be in a position to determine priorities for a grant received from the Department of Housing and Urban Development. Furthermore, the success of *La Raza Unida Party* in Crystal City would spur the organization of Texas Chicanos in other counties.

Chicanos have been increasingly involved in politics since the end of World War II. New organizations have emerged committed to the tenet that politics is the most effective social instrument for improvement. Working to unify the Mexican American vote and use it as a lever to force politicians to be responsive to Mexican American needs, organizations like the Mexican American Political Association, the Political Association of Spanish-Speaking Organizations, the American Coordinating Council of Political Education, and the GI Forum have made valuable inroads in creating Chicano political awareness. In California alone, upwards of a half million new Mexican American voters were registered in the fifteen years between 1950 and 1965.[6] Politically, the "sleeping giant" was becoming a force to be reckoned with.

In 1960 *barrio* leaders brought out a record attendance at the polls for the Democratic party after a highly intense and colorful "Viva Kennedy" campaign. Yet, in 1966 the Democratic party, which had long considered the Mexican American vote "in the bag," learned that the Chicano voter had a mind of his own. Waggoner Carr, Attorney General of Texas running for a Senate seat on the Democratic ticket, met defeat after refusing to meet with the Rio Grande Valley farm workers. The state's Mexican American voters cast their support for the Republican incumbent, Sen. John Tower. In Arizona, another Democrat, the incumbent governor Sam Goddard, lost his office in the state capitol when he alienated his Mexican American supporters. This rumbling of Chicano independence spilled over into the presidential election year of 1968 when Hubert Humphrey lost the state of California because of the party switch of *barrio* voters.

Throughout the Southwest in the sixties, Chicanos were registering, voting, and even running for office. Rodolfo "Corky" Gonzales ran for mayor in Denver. Reies Tijerina was a gubernatorial candidate in New Mexico until being ruled off the ballot. In the East Los Angeles *barrio,* community leaders were running for local offices. More and more, Chicanos were turning to politics as a way to improve conditions. At the organizational conference of *La Raza Unida* held in San Antonio on January 6, 1968, the principal speaker, Dr. Ernesto Galarza, a scholar and writer, stressed that if Mexican Americans are ever to achieve their political, social, and economic goals they must develop meaningful community organizations, and that politics should come first.[7] Echoing the same thoughts, Mario Compean, chairman of the Mexican American Youth Organization (MAYO), in

---

[6]Stan Steiner, "Chicano Power," *New Republic* (June 20, 1970), p. 17.
[7]*La Raza Unida* has scored several impressive political victories. For an overview of the organization and a good introduction to its birth, the reader can consult the article "Mexican-Americans and La Raza," *The Christian Century* (March 5, 1969).

addressing a May 4, 1970, mass meeting said, "I think we Chicanos will never have anything that means anything until we have political power."[8]

For some Mexican Americans, political power means functioning through the established political system. For others, and the number is growing, it means forming an independent Chicano party to serve Chicano needs. Crystal City is a good example of this second view, and the philosophy can be summed up in the words of Crystal City's school board president, José Angel Gutierrez. Addressing the May 4, 1970, MAYO meeting in San Antonio, he emphasized "that mexicanos need to be in control of their destiny. They need to make their own decisions. We need to make the decisions that are going to affect our brothers and maybe our children. We have been complacent for too long."[9]

[8]*La Raza Unida Party in Texas*, p. 9, reproduced from *The Militant* (June 19, 1970).
[9]*Ibid.*, p. 12.

7

THE FARM WORKERS

MIGRANT

EACH SPRING, thousands of trucks, pickups, converted school-buses, dust-worn automobiles, and practically anything else capable of transporting human beings over a long distance leave places like Florida and California, New Mexico and Arizona, and the hot, dusty borderlands of southern Texas for the agricultural heartlands of the United States. It is an annual migration, a calling of sorts which prompts an undetermined number of migrant farm workers to leave their homes to harvest the nation's crops.[10] Migrant farm labor is seasonal. Most of its workers are from Spanish-speaking backgrounds, the majority being Mexican Americans from Texas.[11] It is grueling and often unrewarding work, and frequently an entire family must labor in the fields to make ends meet. At the end of a season which

[10]The figures given for the number of migrant farm workers vary widely. For example, Stan Steiner in *La Raza: The Mexican Americans* places the number in 1969 at 200,000. In *Migrant: Agricultural Workers in America's Northeast,* on the other hand, William Friedland and Dorothy Nelkin put the number in 1971 at a vague 400,000 to 2,000,000. Other sources do little to clear this up.

[11]Dr. Myrtle R. Reul, School of Social Work, Michigan State University, East Lansing, Michigan. From a speech, "Sociocultural Patterns Among Michigan Migrant Farm Workers," delivered at the Farm Labor Family Living Workshop, March 27, 1967, Kellogg Center, Michigan State University, East Lansing, Michigan.

has seen the typical migrant family working the crops from the borderlands to the northernmost states and back again, the family often has not earned enough money to see them through the winter and they must start the following season in the red.

It is a slavery of sorts. A bondage. An individual is usually not a migrant farm worker entirely by choice. Often he is undereducated and unskilled. He may be unable to get a job where he lives. And in most cases he is merely following a pattern established by his parents and reinforced by his peers. In a sense the migrant farm worker leaves each spring and returns each fall because he knows nothing else—he is trapped in a way of life without viable alternatives.

MIGRANT HISTORY. The history of the migrant farm worker is intertwined with the history of the United States. The Mexican Revolution of 1910 sent scores of refugees northward across the border. Most of these refugees escaping the poverty and insecurity of their Latin homeland were illiterate and unskilled *peones* (laborers) who hoped for nothing more than the opportunity to scratch out a living in their "neighbor to the north." Ironically, this period of flight roughly paralleled a period of surging prosperity and growth for agricultural holdings in the United States. Technological innovations in the U.S. canning industry, the development of refrigerated boxcars, and improved irrigation projects in the Southwest stimulated the expansion of agricultural interests. All this coupled with immigration restrictions against Orientals and the outbreak of World War I, which siphoned away American farm labor, dramatically increased the need for farm workers. The infant agri-business found in the Mexican refugees a handy—and cheap—source of supply. At that point, history introduced the institution of migrant farm labor.

This institution became firmly entrenched during the twenties. The Industrial Revolution had drastically altered American life. Within a comparatively short span of time America had changed from a rural to an urban society. The city had offered excitement, a glittering alternative to the harsh and lonely life in rural America. Workers and small farm owners had abandoned the soil and emigrated to the cities in droves. Cities had mushroomed, and the demands for food to feed the surging populations had doubled and redoubled. The decade following 1910 had seen Mexican immigrants filling the places abandoned by Anglo workers, and the twenties continued this trend. By 1930 over a million Mexicans had immigrated to the United States and constituted the majority of the work force in agriculture, mining and railroads throughout the Southwest.

Then, as the twenties drew to an end, the stock market sounded its apoplectic note. The Great Depression settled over the nation, its grim face turning on the Mexican immigrant. The migrant farm laborer was caught in economic conditions beyond his control. As Anglos had fled the farms for the economic security of the city, they suddenly found themselves looking back to the farm as rising unemployment began taking its toll. Mexican farm laborers began finding themselves displaced by Anglo farm laborers. To make matters worse, the "Dust Bowl" crisis which devastated nearly a hundred million acres of land in the southern Great Plains region drove thousands of "Okies" westward. In response to the acute job shortages, the U.S. government put into operation a massive repatriation program to return Mexican laborers to their homeland. The program created much bitterness between the two countries and led to many unjustifiable deportations.

As World War II pulled Anglo farm workers from the fields, Mexican immigrants again replaced them. The *bracero* program and the surge of "wetbacks" filled agricultural jobs primarily with people of Mexican descent. As migrant labor had become an institution in the twenties, Mexican and Mexican American migrant labor became an institution in the forties.

MIGRANT LIFE. The majority of migrant workers in the United States follow one of three migrant streams. The first stream originates in Florida and follows a northward path through the states of the Atlantic Seaboard. The northernmost trajectory of this stream—after beans have been picked in New York and apples, tomatoes, peppers, and asparagus in New Jersey—is New Hampshire, after which the migrants turn south and work their way back to Florida. The second stream fans out from southern Texas and includes a region stretching from Oregon to Ohio, as far north as North Dakota and Minnesota, and through the Gulf States. The third stream, originating in the hotlands of New Mexico and Arizona, moves westward into California and northward through the valleys of the Coast Range into Oregon and Washington.[12]

Life for the migrants who follow these streams is an ambivalent experience at best. On the one hand, many migratory farm workers take pride in their labor. They come primarily from agricultural backgrounds. They know the fields, know what has to be done, and are good at their work. On the other hand, they are faced with the sociological implications of their profession.

The most severe problem facing the migrant worker is that of poverty. Michael Smith, former staff attorney for the U.S. Commission on Civil Rights, prepared a report on farm workers for the civil rights hearings held in San Antonio, Texas, December 9-14, 1968. When he testified before the commission on the morning of December 12, Smith said: "By almost every standard the 3 million or so farm workers in this country constitute its most disadvantaged occupational class. Their extremely poor compensation and high unemployment rate are reflected in the annual migration of over 450,000 persons who find it necessary to travel to other States seeking seasonal employment."[13] And, he went on to add, "The gap between agricultural and nonagricultural wages has continually widened since World War II."[14] Truman Moore in *The Slaves We Rent* said, "The migrants are not just 'statistically' poor. Neither are they statistically hungry or cold. The poverty of the migrant is the old-fashioned kind. It is to be without food, without clothes, without shelter, and without hope in this world."[15]

According to a 1969 report to the National Board of the National Sharecroppers Fund delivered by Fay Bennett ("The Condition of Farm Workers and Small Farmers in 1969"), the average hourly wage of the migrant worker was $1.33. In the

[12]C.E. Bishop, *Farm Labor in the United States* (Columbia University, 1967), p. 27, citing "The Current Situation of the Hired Farm Labor Force," by Gladys Bowles.

[13]Hearing Before the United States Commission on Civil Rights Held at Our Lady of the Lake College, San Antonio, Texas, December 9-14, 1968. U.S. Government Printing Office, Washington, D.C., p. 396.

[14]*Ibid.*, p. 397.

[15]Truman Moore, *The Slaves We Rent* (New York: Random House, 1965), p. xi.

same year, the wages per worker man-hour in manufacturing was $3.27. Stan Steiner in *La Raza: the Mexican Americans* explained, "In recent years, these migrants averaged little over $1,100 annually from field work. And they were lucky to add $600 from odd jobs, off season."[16]

Out of this poverty stems a host of related problems. Many states have wholly inadequate legislation or no legislation at all affecting living and working standards. Those states that do are often lax in enforcement. And as committee after committee meets to discuss conditions in labor camps, they uncover such conditions as polluted drinking water, no toilet facilities, poor garbage and refuse collection, overcrowding, insect- and rodent-infested housing, and inadequate heating, ventilation, and sanitary conditions within the living quarters. All this, of course, leads to the increased likelihood of communicable diseases. As Truman Moore related, "The migrant child is prone to scurvy, rickets, kwashiorkor—a severe protein deficiency . . . the migrant child is also prey to a host of diseases now rare in the nonmigrant world: smallpox, diphtheria, and whooping cough."[17] Migrant mothers tend to regard chronic head colds, skin eruptions, and other such conditions in children as normal, explained Louisa Shotwell in *The Harvesters: the Story of the Migrant People*. Speaking of prevalent ills among the migrants, she said:

> There is the inevitable impetigo and a variety of other skin troubles, including a kind known in the north as "Florida sores." There is a nutritional type of anemia; scurvy; pellagra; rickets; febrile tonsillitis; copious nasal discharge; asthma; intestinal parasites; dysentery; diarrhea, both infant and in epidemics involving the whole family, causing dehydration and sometimes, especially among the younger children, death; inflammation of lymphatic glands; orthopedic defects; congenital heart conditions; vision and hearing defects."[18]

[16]Stan Steiner, *La Raza: the Mexican Americans* (New York: Harper, 1969), p. 248.

[17]Moore, *Slaves We Rent*, p. 57.

[18]Louisa R. Shotwell, *The Harvesters: the Story of the Migrant People*, (Garden City: Doubleday, 1961), p. 143.

In 1969 the Michigan Civil Rights Commission released a report stating their findings in a 1968 study of the migrant population in this state, which is the third largest user of migrant labor. Among its conclusions were these:

1. The migrant population is being excluded from full participation in the life of our society.
2. The present network of laws, policies and practices traps migrants economically and politically.
3. The migrants' position is substantially damaged by lack of adequate housing, minimal social and health services and reasonable educational benefits.[19]

Meanwhile, other agencies have voiced their concerns over the conditions affecting migrant workers. Agencies such as the California State Health Department, the National Safety Council, the Bureau of Labor Standards, and the Department of Health, Education, and Welfare have repeatedly warned that migrant families are exposed to shocking conditions. Children are illegally employed; workers in the field are subjected to dangerously high levels of pesticides and other farm chemicals; migrant laborers are in many states exempted from unemployment and disability compensations, as well as fair-labor standards; accidents happen at an uncommonly high rate; and incidents of malnutrition, illiteracy, welfare dependency, and physical disability continue to soar.

Overriding these concerns is a central concern felt by most migrant workers—fear. Despite the hazards of farm labor, and despite the unpleasantry associated with migrant living, the migrant farm worker still fears for his job, for his economic future. Armando Rendon in a magazine article entitled "How Much Longer . . . the Long Road?", which appeared in the Summer, 1968, issue of *Civil Rights Digest,* explained, "The fear that dominates the migrant is that of losing a job, of not finding a job available that he had last year because of mechanization, demise of a farm, or arriving too late for the first good pickings."[20]

[19] *1969 Report and Recommendations,* "A Field Study of Migrant Workers in Michigan," Michigan Civil Rights Commission, Lansing, Michigan, pp. 1-8.
[20] Burma, *Mexican-Americans in the United States,* p. 194, citing A.

Thus, the migrant worker is placed in a peculiar situation. His future is bleak. Harvest mechanization is gradually replacing the need for human harvesters. Yet, he remains unskilled in other jobs. In order to survive, he must give up part of his heritage and learn new skills to enable him to move into nonagricultural industries.

THE BRACERO PROGRAM

World War II created an acute shortage of farm labor in the United States. Late in the spring of 1942, U.S. officials opened negotiations with the Mexican government for the temporary use of Mexican agricultural workers. The agreement they arrived at and rather cautiously signed that summer (August 4) put into operation the badly needed but, as it turned out, overextended *bracero* program. A similar attempt at importing temporary farm labor from south of the border had been tried in the previous World War with moderate success, but also with wholly unforeseen ramifications. Rather than return to Mexico where poverty was guaranteed, these early *braceros* chose to remain in the United States, where at least the poverty was not as severe and where there was more chance for betterment. When the Great Depression struck, thousands of these *braceros* and their families elected to return to their homeland, flooding the Republic of Mexico with an unexpected and, in view of the circumstances, unwanted labor mass. As jobs became even more scarce in the United States, anti-alien sentiment mounted and authorities repatriated thousands more Mexicans to their native land. The massive return migration and the realities of forced repatriation strained relations between the two countries. Thus, when representatives again met at the conference table five months after the Japanese attack on Pearl Harbor, they did so with restrained enthusiasm and the resolve not to repeat the same mistake.

The 1942 *bracero* agreement incorporated conditions and restraints for the protection of the United States, Mexico, the Mexican agricultural worker, and the American farm worker

Rendon, "How Much Longer . . . the Long Road?", *Civil Rights Digest* (Summer, 1968).

upon his return from the war effort. These included the following stipulations:

1. no labor was to be recruited unless the grower could prove that such labor was necessary;
2. all work was to be agricultural and a written contract was to be used in the hiring;
3. no incentives nor inducements could be used to encourage the *bracero* to remain in the United States;
4. there was to be no racial discrimination;
5. transportation costs were to be assumed by the U.S. government;
6. wages were to be equal those of the average in the area, with a minimum wage set at thirty cents per hour;
7. adequate housing and sanitary facilities were to be provided;
8. a fund was to be established for each *bracero* in which ten percent of his earnings was set aside to be drawn from on his return to Mexico;
9. work was to be guaranteed for three-quarters of the contract period; and
10. *braceros* were to be exempt from military duty.[21]

During the war years and up to 1947, the *bracero* program worked efficiently, proving beneficial to American growers. Beginning in 1948, however, it came under increasing attack from politicians and domestic workers. Even though the program supplied adequate labor, growers continued hiring "wetbacks" illegally immigrating to the United States. They could hire these illegal aliens for less and avoid the complications and expenses of governmental recruitment (growers had to pay a $15 contracting fee and post a $25 bond for each *bracero*); and with the number of "wetbacks" increasing each year, growers had a ready supply of labor.[22] The continued use of *braceros* and "wetbacks" removed thousands of jobs from American farm workers. These farm workers, then, were forced to either move to urban centers or remain and scratch out a living in any way possible, faced with the despair of unemployment, poverty, and starvation.

[21]Ernesto Galarza, *Merchants of Labor: The Mexican Bracero Story* (Santa Barbara, Calif.: McNally & Loftin, 1964), pp. 47-48.
[22]*Ibid.*, p. 57.

In 1954 the government attacked the problem of illegal immigration into the United States. "Operation Wetback," initiated by the U.S. Immigration and Naturalization Service, accounted for the removal of over a million illegals that year.[23] Yet, conditions for the American farm worker remained little changed. He still had to compete with the *bracero* for agricultural jobs.

Despite protests, the *bracero* program was renewed periodically. In 1951, Public Law 78 transferred responsibility for the control and operation from the grower to the Department of Agriculture. Subsequent ammendments were attached in 1954, 1955, and 1959. By the early sixties, opposition to the program reached new proportions, and in 1963 the Secretary of Agriculture announced its termination. The following December, 1964, the *bracero* program officially ended.

THE CALIFORNIA GRAPE STRIKE

PHASE 1. The Great Central Valley of California stretches like a long, flat ribbon between two walls of mountains, the Sierra Nevada range to the east, and the Coast Range to the west. The land is flat and arid, but modern irrigation techniques have harnessed the fertile soil for man, making the Central Valley California's most important agricultural region. Agribusiness in the Valley represents a $4 billion-a-year industry with an output of nearly half of the nation's fruit and vegetables.[24] Cotton is the region's chief crop, but the Valley also produces more fruit than any other state in the union. Important in the fruit industry is the production of table and wine grapes. The Central Valley supplies most of the nation's grapes and grape products. There, the vineyards of Gallo, Paul Masson, Schenley, DiGiorgio, Guimarra, and Dispoto are located. And there, in the Great Central Valley of California, the longest agricultural strike in history occurred.

The California Grape Strike formally began on September 8, 1965, when the Agricultural Workers Organizing Committee (AWOC) called a general strike of its Filipino workers against

[23]*Ibid.*, p. 70.
[24]Burma, *Mexican-Americans in the U.S.*, p. 189, citing A. Rendon, "How Much Longer . . . the Long Road?"

the vineyards around Delano. A few months earlier, the Filipino farm workers, demanding the same wage scale as the Mexican *braceros*, had struck the growers in the Coachella Valley on the edge of the Mojave Desert. The growers there had settled within ten days, raising wages from $1.10 to $1.40 an hour.[25] When the pickers had moved north into the San Joaquin Valley, they faced the same problem. Thus, AWOC called for its second strike vote of that year against the growers around Delano. Almost immediately, the Delano growers retaliated by hiring scab labor, neutralizing the strength of the Filipino strike. AWOC was in a quandary. Unless they gained the support of the Mexican American farm workers in the area, their strike would fail.

Early in the strike, Larry Itliong, the tough Filipino organizer, asked for a meeting with Cesar Chavez, the leader of the predominantly Mexican American National Farm Workers Association (NFWA). NFWA had been formed in 1962 after Chavez had resigned from Saul Alinsky's Community Service Organization to form his own farm workers union. By 1965 Chavez had managed to recruit over 1700 families and the same year struck the rose growers around McFarland. However, the "Strike of Roses" had been small compared with the strike Itliong wanted him to join.

After the meeting, Chavez had serious misgivings about pledging his union's support. Relations between the AWOC and the NFWA had not been good in previous years. At the member level, racial antagonism existed between the Filipinos and Mexican Americans. Besides, Chavez suspected NFWA was not yet ready for a major strike. A failure at this point in NFWA's growth could wipe out his organization. On the other hand, if he refused, the grape strike would undoubtedly fail and his position as *caudillo* (leader) would be seriously weakened.[26] By September 16, Mexican Independence Day, he had made his decision and called for a meeting of his union members. In an impassioned plea, he asked for a strike vote. The *campesinos* (farm workers) answered unanimously. *Huelga! Huelga! Huelga!* The California Grape Strike was on.

---

[25]Steiner, *La Raza*, p. 282.
[26]John Gregory Dunne, *Delano: The Story of the California Grape Strike* (New York: Farrar, Straus & Giroux, 1967), p. 79.

NFWA joined the strike on September 20, its main emphasis centering around Delano. Pickets were strategically placed at major growers, while smaller vineyards were allowed to operate virtually unaffected. This strategy allowed Chavez to keep a contingency of farm workers employed while the main thrust of the strike centered on breaking the resistance of the larger, more influential growers. If DiGiorgio and Schenley, Chavez reasoned, responded to the strikers' demands, the smaller growers would logically follow suit.[27]

The strike was ineffective for the first three months.[28] Vineyards used "green-carders" and scab labor imported from other parts of California and Texas, while NFWA and AWOC struggled with legal entanglements, morale problems, and economic impotency. Law enforcement officials maintained constant surveillance of the picket lines. Local judges issued injunctions restricting union activity. Tension mounted, leading to outbreaks of hostility. Growers sprayed pickets with insecticides and fertilizers. Strikers punctured tires and damaged cars of scab laborers. Minor skirmishes erupted involving strikers and foremen, pickets and police officials. A psychological game of action, reaction, counterreaction evolved.

Economically, NFWA and AWOC suffered heavily. Strikers had to exist on $5.00 a week from the strike fund. They faced shortages of food, clothing, housing, and medical care. Frustration and the threat of defeat stalked them. The strike was failing and monetary resources were too slim to sustain a long campaign. Chavez appealed for help, and organizations like the California Migrant Ministry and Walter Reuther's United Auto Workers responded. Individual contributions and contributions from various agencies began filtering into the depleted strike fund. Doctors and nurses began contributing their time and medical supplies. The Student Non-violent Coordinating Committee sent personnel down from Berkeley to help with the picketing. Church groups, social agencies, and private businessmen shipped in food and clothing. The outside world was beginning to respond and identify with the plight of the farm worker.

[27]*Ibid.,* pp. 80-85.
[28]Matt S. Meier and Feliciano Rivera, *The Chicanos—A History of Mexican Americans* (New York: Hill and Wang, 1972), p. 265.

Yet, the strike was failing despite outside help. Chavez responded by concentrating a boycott against Schenley products, reasoning that economic pressures might drive this major grower into a settlement. He sent representatives to thirteen major cities to organize boycott centers. However, the effects of this initial boycott were negligible and Chavez realized the need to publicize the strike to gain public support.

On March 17, 1966, Chavez began a 250-mile march from Delano to the state capitol at Sacramento. It took twenty-five days, and only fifty-seven marchers completed the journey. Aside from gaining a small flourish of publicity, the march ended in failure, for the man they had principally gone to see, Governor Pat Brown, was out of his office on vacation. So far, everything Chavez had tried had proven unsuccessful. Then, a strange twist of fate dramatically altered the situation. Officials of the Schenley Corporation, hearing a false rumor that the Los Angeles Bartenders Local planned on boycotting Schenley products because of the strike, notified Chavez that they were ready for talks. In April, Schenley officially recognized NFWA as the bargaining agent for its pickers.

PHASE 2. Now free to concentrate their efforts on the giant DiGiorgio Corporation, NFWA met opposition from Jimmy Hoffa's Teamsters' Union, who had come to Delano to organize the workers of DiGiorgio's Sierra Vista farm for the Teamsters. The Teamsters had originally backed NFWA, even supporting the Schenley strike, but with Hoffa on trial for tampering with union funds, the resultant leadership struggle was apparently responsible for casting the farms around Delano as fair game. DiGiorgio, feeling increasing NFWA pressure, opened negotiations with the Teamsters. Chavez, however, protested this action vigorously, and DiGiorgio finally consented to recognize a vote of his workers in determining union representation.

On June 24, 1966, DiGiorgio opened the polls. But Chavez, disagreeing with the proceedings, asked the Sierra Vista farm workers to boycott the election. Nearly half did, and NFWA refused to recognize the Teamsters' victory. Four days later, California Governor Pat Brown appointed a commissioner to investigate the election. The commissioner recommended that a new election be held on August 30th.

What had prompted Governor Brown to act was the

particularly shameful treatment of Chavez and some of his workers. Several workers of the Sierra Vista farm had contacted Chavez and expressed their fear of harassment by security police and police dogs. Chavez accompanied the workers back to the farm to investigate these charges. No sooner had they stepped onto the DiGiorgio property than a security guard placed them under citizen's arrest for trespassing. Chavez and the workers were stripped of their clothing, chained together, and transported to jail. The public indignation over this and increasing public awareness of conditions facing the farm worker added new impetus to the NFWA organization, renewing the morale of the strikers.

In August, sorely in need of money and organizing strength, Chavez merged NFWA with AWOC and joined the AFL-CIO. Under a new name, the United Farm Workers Organizing Committee (UFWOC), Chavez continued the strike. On August 30th the promised election took place, and UFWOC won the right to represent the DiGiorgio field workers. The following year the Teamsters negotiated a pact with UFWOC which allowed the Teamsters to organize processing plants and warehouses and UFWOC to organize field workers. Immediately following this agreement, Paul Masson, Gallo, and other vineyards agreed to open talks with the farm workers union.

After the DiGiorgio victory, Chavez concentrated the full force of his strike against the largest table-grape grower in America, the Guimarra Vineyards. He had been striking Guimarra since 1965 with no success, and even under increased pressure, Guimarra failed to respond. Out of desperation, Chavez issued a plea to boycott Guimarra products. When it became evident to UFWOC officials that Guimarra was labeling its grapes with over a hundred different labels to bypass the boycott, Chavez asked consumers to stop buying any California table-grapes.

As the deadlock continued, incidents of striker violence dramatically increased. Property damage, beatings, and overt hostility threatened to lead the strike away from Chavez's professed philosophy of nonviolence. To halt this, and also to show the growers that he meant business, Chavez entered upon a twenty-five-day fast. Farm workers from throughout the Valley and southern California came to see and pay homage to their *caudillo*. Prominent Mexican Americans as well as Anglos made pilgrimages to the garage on Forty Acres, paying tribute to the ideals and beliefs of the man who had unselfishly devoted his life to the betterment of his people. The fast was a success. The strikers rallied around his cry for nonviolence, and publicity moved the nation to take the table-grape boycott seriously.[29]

In the Spring of 1970, feeling the economic pressure of the boycott, growers in the Coachella Valley signed a union agreement with Chavez. Their crates of table-grapes, bearing UFWOC's black Aztec eagle emblem, were immune from the boycott. Finally, in July, the mighty Guimarra Vineyards capitulated. The California Grape Strike was over.

[29]Dunne, *Delano*, pp. 185-186.

8
CHICANO LEADERS

CESAR

FORTY ACRES IS A CONGLOMERATION OF DUST, unfinished construction, withered sapplings, and dreams. It lies outside Delano, California, off the Garces Highway, and is the site of the proposed union headquarters of the United Farm Workers Organizing Committee (UFWOC). It is the dream of many men, but especially of Cesar Chavez, whose unselfish example molded a new image for the Mexican American.[30]

Cesar Estrada Chavez was born in Yuma, Arizona, in 1926. He lived his first ten years on a small farm near the Colorado River. When his father lost the farm in the mid-thirties, Cesar and his family joined the migrant stream working the crops from Arizona to California. Their new home became a combination of an ancient car and various migrant camps until the family settled in San Jose, in a grim barrio called *Sal Si Puedes* (get out if you can). It was in San Jose, when Cesar had reached thirteen, that his father and uncle joined the CIO, which had been organizing workers in the dried-fruit industry. Union meetings were frequently held in the Chavez home, and this union activity made a deep impression on young Cesar.

A few years later Cesar left home. In Delano he met and married a young Mexican American named Helen, after which he returned to San Jose. There he found a job picking apricots, and

[30]Dunne, *Delano,* p. 68.

there he met Father Donald McDonnell, a Catholic priest. A warm friendship grew between the two men. They often spent long evenings together discussing social justice, Catholicism, and the farm labor movement.[31] Soon after, Father McDonnell introduced Chavez to Fred Ross, an organizer for the Community Service Organization (CSO), which had been formed by Saul Alinsky to help the poor organize power blocs. Ross, immediately impressed by Chavez, persuaded him to join the CSO. And for the next ten years, Cesar worked among Mexican Americans in San Jose, Decoto, Oakland, and the San Joaquin Valley.

During his ten-year apprenticeship with the CSO, Chavez learned many successful organizing techniques. In addition, he learned the vital ingredient for his later success—a leader must share the life style and discomfort of those he hopes to lead.[32] By 1958 his skill and determination earned him a general directorship with the National CSO. However, as a national director he became disillusioned. His promotion had moved him into the organizational bureaucracy. He no longer dealt directly with the victims of poverty but rather with a middle-class core. Meetings were held in expensive motels, dinners in elaborate restaurants. Chavez lasted four years, but they were four frustrating years. Much of his sympathy was clearly with the farm workers, yet he felt that the CSO was basically ignoring their problems. He resigned his position in 1962 after a farm-union proposal he had drafted was voted down.

His CSO experience behind him, Chavez moved to Delano to organize his own farm workers union. He invested his personal savings of $1200 and three difficult years to form the National Farm Workers Association (NFWA). Visiting fields during the days, traveling from town to town in the evenings, talking to hundreds of *campesinos,* and mimeographing thousands of cards and flyers advertising union meetings, Chavez managed to create a union strong enough for recognition. On May 3, 1965, the infant NFWA struck the powerful Mount Arbor Nurseries, the largest grower of roses in California. Four days later the grower came to an agreement with the new union.

[31]Steiner, *La Raza,* p. 313.
[32]*Ibid.,* p. 314.

Later that year, on September 8, 2,000 Filipino grape pickers, members of the Agricultural Workers Organizing Committee (AWOC), struck the vineyards around Delano. The growers retaliated by hiring scab labor, mostly Mexicans. Larry Itliong, the chief AWOC organizer in Delano, knew that the strike would fail unless he could get Chavez to join him. The two men met and agreed, and on Mexican Independence Day, September 16, Chavez called for a strike vote from his fledgling NFWA. The *Huelga* was on, and would prove to be the longest agricultural strike in history.[33]

The California Grape Strike lasted nearly five years. During its course the nation became involved in a grape boycott which extended the plight of the farm worker into the homes and kitchens of families throughout the United States. New attention was focused on agriculture and especially upon the Mexican American worker. Cesar Chavez became a folk hero to millions of Americans and a living saint to the members of La Raza. Yet, throughout this new era he maintained a humility and earthiness which kept him endeared to the members of his farm workers union. In a classic manner he led a Pilgrimage to Sacramento to see the governor, but also to show the unity of the strikers. Midway through the strike he endured a twenty-three-day fast to reaffirm his nonviolent stand, a fast which left him bedridden for several months. He was jailed. He was visited by men like Robert Kennedy and Walter Reuther. He turned down bribes. He also turned down honors, for essentially he is just a simple man with a dream, a dream of seeing pride and dignity restored to the farm worker—plus a living wage.

EL TIGRE

On Monday, July 26, 1971, Reies Lopez Tijerina stepped from the federal penitentiary at El Paso, Texas, after serving 775 days for his part in the siege of the Echo Amphitheater in New Mexico's Kit Carson National Forest and for "aiding in the burning" of a U.S. Forest Service sign. Returning immediately to Albuquerque, New Mexico, the home of his famous *Alianza Federal de Mercedes*, Tijerina proclaimed his intention to study

---

[33] *Ibid.*, pp. 282-283.

"the history and life of justice in the world." Undoubtedly encouraging his decision to research *justice* was a parole condition banning his active leadership as an official of the *Alianza;* however, the search for justice has been a dominant theme in Tijerina's life. It pushed him into religion as a minister; it pushed him to walk from Illinois to Texas to understand what the biblical prophets of justice had experienced in their journeys; it pushed him into Mexico and Spain to study Spanish land grants; and it pushed him to challenge the U.S. government for the rightful ownership of vast tracts of land in the Southwest.

Tijerina was born on September 21, 1926, in Fall City, Texas. Much of his childhood, like the childhood of so many Mexican Americans, was spent on the back of a truck following the crops across the Midwest. At eighteen, he enrolled in the Assembly of God Bible Institute at Ysleta, Texas. Although he did not graduate (he was suspended for dating), he became a Pentecostal preacher and for ten years followed the migrant workers from crop to crop, state to state. The years of Tijerina's ministry were characterized by extreme self-denial. He felt that only through reliving the asceticism of the holy men could he preach their words. This led him to make his epic walk through the Midwest into Texas and to forego all luxuries, and even some necessities, in his personal life. In 1950 he fell into discord with the Pentecostal Church for his unorthodox behavior and because he had begun discouraging his followers from paying tithes. The same year he lost his ministerial credentials, becoming a nondenominational minister.[34]

In the mid-fifties, Tijerina and his followers purchased 160 acres of land in Arizona to form an utopian community. The *Valle de Paz* (Valley of Peace) lasted only a short time. Local harassment and vandalism drove the commune members away.

A couple of years later, in 1957, Tijerina was accused by Arizona authorities of driving the "getaway car" for his brother's escape from the Pinal County jail. For the next three years Tijerina eluded both the police and FBI. His flight carried

[34]For a well-written, in-depth account of Tijerina's life, see *Tijerina and the Courthouse Raid* by Peter Nabokov (Albuquerque: University of New Mexico, 1969).

him into Mexico, where he spent a year studying the old Spanish land grants. In 1960, legally vulnerable, he went to New Mexico to continue his research. From libraries in Mexico City and from old maps and documents produced by his followers in New Mexico, he held evidence that millions of acres of land had been virtually stolen from the original landowners. Legal and quasi-legal chicanery, the burning of records and deeds, and other questionable practices had transferred ownership of land guaranteed the Hispano population by the Treaty of Guadalupe Hidalgo following the Mexican-American War. In 1963, Tijerina formed the *Alianza Federal de Mercedes* "to organize and acquaint the Heirs of all Spanish land grants covered by the Guadalupe Treaty."[35]

The three years between 1963 and 1966 were used by Tijerina to organize the *Alianza.* In 1966 he visited Spain to gather more evidence, and upon his return to the United States he confronted New Mexico's governor Jack Campbell with a petition asking for "a full investigation of the issue." When Campbell failed to respond, Tijerina and the *Alianzas* took over Echo Amphitheater, a national campground in the Kit Carson National Forest. There, the *Alianza* proclaimed the existence of the independent state of *San Joaquin del Rio de Chama.* A mayor, city officials, and marshalls were elected, U.S. Forest Rangers were arrested for trespassing, and armed guards patrolled the campground until they were dispersed by federal, state, and FBI officials. Tijerina and four *Alianzas* were charged on counts of assault, converting governmental property to private use, and conspiracy.

The following year Tijerina again found himself the subject of a police chase. On June 5, 1967, a group of *Alianzas* descended upon the Rio Arriba County Courthouse to place under citizen's arrest the District Attorney of Sante Fe, Rio Arriba, and Los Alamos counties. The armed raid left two men wounded, and the state police, national guard, and FBI scoured the nearby hills for Tijerina, who had been named the leader of the raid. This time when caught he was charged with kidnapping, impersonating an officer, and assault.

Tijerina was found innocent of the charges brought against

[35]Nabokov, *Tijerina*, p. 211.

him for the courthouse raid, and for the next two years he traveled throughout the Southwest to gain support for his land grant movement. On June 8, 1969, he was seized by the New Mexico State Police. His bail had been revoked for the Echo Amphitheater charges, whereupon he was remanded to the Federal Penitentiary at El Paso.

CORKY

Rodolfo "Corky" Gonzales, who left a world of fame and glamour for the world of sacrifice, frustration, and struggle, was born in Denver, Colorado, on June 18, 1928. His father was a Mexican emigrant who labored in the fields and coal mines of southern Colorado, and Corky's earliest experiences were tinged with the presence of poverty and hunger. Soon after, his father took the Gonzales family and joined the migrant stream. Corky and his three brothers were thrust into the nomadic life of the Mexican American farm worker, following the crops, changing from community to community, school to school. By the age of ten, Corky fit well into the pattern established by two generations of Mexican immigrants. He worked in the fields alongside his father to help contribute to the meager family income.

Corky, in defiance of statistics which rated him and his fellow Mexican Americans a less than even chance of graduating from high school, worked in a bowling alley and slaughterhouse to finance his education. At the age of sixteen, he received his high school diploma and turned to the world of sports.

By 1947, Corky Gonzales had made his mark in amateur athletics. Showing tenacity and skill in the boxing ring, he won the National A.A.U. featherweight division championship. Turning to professional boxing, he battered out an impressive record. Winning sixty-five out of seventy-five professional bouts, he rose to become the number three contender, as ranked by the National Boxing Association. *Ring Magazine* rated him among the top five boxers in the world in the featherweight class.[36]

Leaving the world of boxing for the world of business, Gonzales and his wife, the former Geraldine Romero, whom he married in 1949, returned to Denver. He entered the surety-

[36]Steiner, *La Raza*, p. 378.

bond business. By 1960 he owned a bail-bond agency and an automobile insurance agency. In his spare time he wrote, and out of this era in his life came his epic poem "I Am Joaquin," a chronicle of self-discovery and of the emasculation of Chicanos by Anglo forces.

Moving more and more towards Chicano activism, he financed the first Chicano newspaper in Denver, *Viva,* which served as an organ for communication and discontent in the *barrio.* [37]   Politically, he ran for the city council and became the first Chicano District Captain in the history of Denver. In the 1960 "Viva Kennedy Campaign," his district turned out a record vote for the Democratic party. Meanwhile, he continued writing poetry and two plays, *The Revolutionist* and *A Cross for Maclovio,* which trace the identity crisis of the modern-day Chicano caste in an Anglicized environment.

When the War on Poverty focused national attention on minority groups and the poor, Gonzales, already a noted lecturer, successful businessman, writer, and minor politician, was appointed to numerous positions. Serving as the Director of the Neighborhood Youth Corps, Chairman of the War on Poverty Board of Denver, member of the Civil Rights Commission, President of the National Community Relations Committee, and member of governing boards of several other anti-poverty programs throughout the Southwest, he came face to face with the Anglo power structure.

After a malicious attack by a Denver-area newspaper which alluded to acts of dishonesty and charged discriminatory management of the poverty programs, Gonzales found himself strangely deserted by his former Anglo friends and associates. The charges and innuendos were proven false, but Gonzales had learned an important lesson: he was a Chicano and it was almost futile to expect any real and meaningful help from Anglo liberals, who continued to view minority group status through Anglicized eyes—the key to Chicano progress was held by Chicano hands. In a scathing letter of resignation, Corky Gonzales left the unreal world of politics and shady compromises and returned to the *barrio* to organize his people at the grass-roots

[37]Armando B. Rendon, *Chicano Manifesto* (New York: Macmillan, 1971), p. 167.

level. It was out of this frustration that in 1965 he founded *La Crusada Para la Justicia,* the Crusade for Justice, which sought equality and dignity for the Chicano through Chicano determination and community control.

9

CHICANO ORGANIZATIONS

THE BROWN BERETS

EARLY IN 1967 the Young Citizens for Community Action was formed in the East Los Angeles *barrio* by David Sanchez, Carlos Móntez, and Ralph Ramírez to serve as a tool for Chicano discontent. Leaning towards militancy, the group soon changed its name to the Young Chicanos for Community Action and opened a coffee house, *La Piranya,* which functioned as a meeting place for members. There, the infant Brown Berets listened to such speakers as H. Rap Brown, Stokely Carmichael, Ron Karenga, Cesar Chavez, and Reies Tijerina discuss social inequality and liberation. From these early influences, and from their own dissatisfaction with conditions affecting Chicanos in a white-oriented society, the youthful members of the YCCA began identifying with Chicano nationalism. Confrontations with the police increased; and late in 1967 the Brown Berets emerged as the radical voice of Mexican Americans across the nation.

At present the Brown Berets claim to have chapters in twenty-eight cities, with their membership instructed to "serve, observe, and protect" Chicano communities from the white power structure.[38] Members are recruited from among *barrio* youth and must observe strict disciplines which include abstain-

---

38Rendon, *Chicano Manifesto,* p. 205.

ing from drugs and excessive drinking, maintaining proper personal hygiene, and attending all Brown Beret activities.

In 1969, David Sanchez, the organization's Prime Minister, produced a manual to act as a guideline for the Brown Beret membership. In it he included a Ten-Point Program outlining the major demands of the Brown Berets. They are the following:

1. The unity of all Chicanos.
2. Bilingual education in schools with Chicano attendance.
3. The inclusion of Chicano history in schools of the five Southwestern states.
4. Civilian police review boards.
5. Police officers serving in a Chicano community must live in that community and speak Spanish.
6. Chicanos whose homes are razed by urban renewal programs must be given job training to enable them to acquire employment which will permit them to build new homes in their *barrios.*
7. A guaranteed annual income of $5000 for all Chicano families.
8. Juries trying Chicanos must be composed equally of members of each race and be of the same socio-economic status as the defendant.
9. Voting literacy tests to be in Spanish for Spanish-speaking citizens and voting rights extending to those who speak only Spanish.
10. The right to keep and bear arms for use against threatening elements from outside the Chicano community.[39]

Like members of the Black Panther Party, the Brown Berets carry identification cards which state and serve as a reminder of their three main objectives—"to serve, observe, and protect." Putting these objectives into practice, the Brown Berets protected Chicano students during the 1968 high school "blow-out" in East Los Angeles. The following year they opened a free medical clinic in the Los Angeles *barrio.* Doctors and nurses donate their own time and provide a variety of services includ-

---

[39]Ruth S. Lamb, *Mexican Americans: Sons of the Southwest* (Claremont, Calif.: Ocelot Press, 1970), pp. 127-128.

ing psychiatric assistance, counseling, child care, and help for drug victims.

MOVIMIENTO ESTUDIANTIL DE CHICANO DE AZTLÁN

In 1968, Chicano students at UCLA formed a dual-purpose organization called the United Mexican American Students (UMAS). It was meant to foster cultural pride in Mexican American students and to encourage Chicanos to express their pride and concerns at the college level.[40] In May of the following year, UMAS participated in a Chicano student forum in Santa Barbara. There, they encouraged the representatives of various Chicano student organizations to unite and form a power unit to further Chicano aims and promote Chicano nationalism. Out of this meeting came the *Movimiento Estudiantil de Chicano de Aztlán* (MECHA).

MECHA is a young organization. It follows the foundation laid by UMAS—cultural pride and unity—and subscribes to the Spiritual Plan of Aztlan set forth by the Crusade for Justice. As a force for nationalism it is rapidly spreading to campuses across the United States, inculcating Chicano students at all levels with the sense of destiny inherent in the Brown Power Movement.

THE POLITICAL ASSOCIATION OF SPANISH-SPEAKING ORGANIZATIONS AND THE AMERICAN COORDINATING COUNCIL OF POLITICAL EDUCATION

Following the election of John F. Kennedy in 1960, Albert Peña, State Chairman of the Viva Kennedy movement in Texas, called together the various Viva Kennedy clubs in order to create a new organization to maintain the Chicano unity they had forged that year. It was Peña's hope that a union of these clubs would form a powerful new tool to advance the political aspirations of Chicanos. What followed his call for unity was a new organization, the Political Association of Spanish-Speaking Organizations (PASO).

PASO has remained basically a Texas force. Its most notable success occurred in the 1963 elections in Crystal City, where it

[40]Lamb, *Sons of the Southwest*, p. 123.

managed to get a Mexican American mayor elected. Other than that, it has worked more or less behind the scenes, conducting voter-registration drives and encouraging Chicanos to become politically aware.[41]

Soon after its creation, PASO moved into Arizona to try to unify Mexican Americans there. It met with little success, but its founding idea was adopted by Arizona Chicanos who formed the American Coordinating Council of Political Education. Although the names are different, PASO and ACCPE have similar aims. They hope to use the Chicano vote as a wedge to further Chicano ends.

THE CRUSADE FOR JUSTICE

With the rallying cry of *venceremos* (we shall overcome), Rodolfo "Corky" Gonzales established in April, 1965, the Crusade for Justice to "secure equality with dignity for the Mexican-Americans and Spanish-named people of the City of Denver, the State of Colorado and the entire Southwest."[42] Acting as a watchdog for Chicano interests, this Denver-based organization has burgeoned since its inception to become a leadership and policy tool for Chicanos throughout the United States. In the areas of civil rights, education, housing, employment, political action, and self-determination, the Crusade for Justice has proven itself a strong voice and a powerful force to help Mexican Americans achieve full citizenship.

The Crusade for Justice realized early that the best opportunity for full citizenship lay in Chicano nationalism. Operating from this premise, the Crusade for Justice began making its weight and the weight of Mexican Americans felt. In education the Crusade for Justice sponsored free schools to revitalize the Chicano identity and culture. They applied pressure on the Denver school system to abandon its traditional Anglo-oriented approach in teaching and include minority contributions in courses as well. Going further, they sponsored a student walk-out in December, 1969, from Denver's West High School to gain a better representation of Chicano teachers and administrators.

---

[41] Meier and Rivera, *The Chicanos,* p. 249.
[42] From the pamphlet "Crusade for Justice," supplied by the Crusade for Justice, 1567 Downing, Denver, Colorado, p. 1.

The Crusade for Justice has opened nursery schools, cultural centers, art galleries, libraries, gymnasiums, and special summer schools and has provided a model for other Chicano communities to follow in their drive for equality.

In the field of employment, the Crusade for Justice has acted as a liaison between management and labor and the business and Chicano communities. In addition to opening employment opportunities for Mexican Americans, it has managed to capture the interest of federal job-training programs.

In the area of Civil Rights the Crusade for Justice has established funds for legal aid and provided access to attorneys. They have adopted community education programs to teach Chicanos their rights under the law.

In other fields such as housing, discrimination, and political action, the Crusade for Justice has been at the forefront, hammering out the twin themes of human rights and Chicano nationalism.

In March of 1969, Corky Gonzales and the Crusade for Justice played host to the Youth Liberation Conference, a meeting of Chicano activists from throughout the Southwest. This conference formally adopted a program designed to achieve Chicano nationalism. Called "The Spiritual Plan of Aztlan" (*El Plan Espiritual De Aztlan*), this program seeks to revitalize the old spirit of the defeated Aztecs. Evoking solidarity, the plan states that Chicanos "must use their nationalism as the key or common denominator for mass mobilization and organization." "We are a Bronze People with a Bronze Culture," the plan proclaims. "Our struggle then must be the control of our Barrios, campos, pueblos, lands, our economy, our culture, and our political life."[43]

THE COMMUNITY SERVICE ORGANIZATION

In 1946, Edward R. Roybal ran for a seat on the Los Angeles city council. He was defeated. This defeat—when a solid Chicano vote would have assured victory—led him to question the unity of his people. Adopting Saul Alinsky's theory that a unified community is a powerful force for progress, Roybal and

---

43 From *"El Plan Espiritual De Aztlan,"* supplied by the Crusade for Justice, Denver, Colorado.

his campaign committee began making preparations for the next election. These preparations included the creation of the Community Service Organization (CSO), which immediately went to the people, getting Chicanos registered to vote and schooling them in the principles of power-bloc voting. When it came time for the 1948 city council election, Roybal, backed by a now-united Chicano community, won handily with a nearly two-to-one margin. Right from the start the CSO showed itself a potent force to combat the unsavory conditions affecting minority groups in the United States.

For the past twenty-five years, the CSO has been an organization dedicated to instilling a sense of self-determination among the Chicano population of the Southwest. Receiving guidance from Fred Ross, the West Coast organizer for Alinsky's Industrial Area Foundation in Chicago, the CSO has promoted three main objectives:

1. to create a sense of civic responsibility;
2. to guarantee constitutional rights for Chicanos;
3. and to coordinate community activities to help the community itself.[44]

Now more than 50,000 strong, the CSO has been active in breaking down discrimination, insuring that the minimum wage law is observed, offering help to migrant workers, promoting consumer education, and sponsoring social services.[45] During the sixties the CSO received a grant from the Office of Economic Opportunity and was able to extend its services, maintaining a staff of field workers in smaller communities throughout the Southwest.

THE GI FORUM

Following World War II, a new battle erupted in the small Texas community of Three Rivers. The fight centered over deposition of the remains of a U.S. infantryman, Felix Longoria, killed in the Philippines. The military had shipped Longoria's remains to his home town. However, Three Rivers' only mortician, acting upon advice of local officials, refused to

[44]Meier and Rivera, *The Chicanos*, p. 245.
[45]*Ibid.*

accept the body for burial in the community's all-white ceme-
tery. The obduracy of the mortician and the city fathers ignited
a fusillade of protest from indignant Chicano war veterans.
Various organizations joined the outcry, trying to pressure the
Texas community into relenting. Throughout that state, and
throughout the United States, individual citizens—even prominent ones like Sen. Lyndon Baines Johnson—raised their voices
against this "basic inhumanity" toward one who had given his
life in the defense of his country.

The forces confronting the Three Rivers' officials lost the
battle—Longoria was buried in the Arlington National Ceme-
tery—but the incident so incensed a Texas physician that a new
battlefront was opened in this war against racism. In Corpus
Christi, Dr. Hector P. Garcia, himself a former combat surgeon,
put out a call for Mexican Americans to unite. And in 1948 the
GI Forum was established.[46]

At first the GI Forum was a small Texas-based organization
aimed at stopping the racism facing Chicano war veterans. It
dealt primarily with the discrimination, and consequently the
inadequate service, affecting Chicanos in veterans hospitals.
Within a short time, however, its goals expanded to include the
attainment of first-class citizenship for all Mexican Americans.
From the veterans hospitals it moved into the schools. Education, the organization felt, was the key to removing the stigma
of second-class citizenship.

The GI Forum has been instrumental in raising money to
create scholarships for Mexican American youngsters. It encourages political and community action and further works to
establish fair employment practices which would benefit all
minority people. Composed primarily of the middle class, it
exerts a strong hand in the whole area of civil rights and
maintains a full-time lobby in Washington. Since 1948 it has
steadily grown more influential and has chapters throughout
most of the United States.

THE MEXICAN AMERICAN YOUTH ORGANIZATION

In May, 1967, José Angel Gutierrez, twenty-six years old,
along with four other Chicano students from St. Mary's College

---

[46]Rendon, *Chicano Manifesto*, p. 117.

in San Antonio, founded the Mexican American Youth Organization (MAYO). Its major aim was to change the educational system of the Southwest by:

1. creating courses dealing with Mexican history and culture;
2. changing the Anglo stereotype of Mexican Americans as being capable only of menial labor;
3. preparing Mexican American youth for professional positions; and
4. changing the ruling of Texas school systems which forbade the speaking of Spanish on school grounds.[47]

The youthful organization made its first impact on March 30, 1968, when it helped lead a Palm Sunday march protesting the ousting of a VISTA project from Val Verde County, Texas. This project, the Minority Mobilization Program, had been composed mainly of Chicanos and had emphasized minority involvement in community activities. Climbing onto the steps of the county courthouse, Gutierrez delivered the "Del Rio Manifesto," which warned the Texans of the social upheaval which could result from their decision. The message also carried a warning to the United States Congress emphasizing the jeopardy all volunteer service programs faced if the decision of the Val Verde County officials was allowed to stand.

MAYO enjoyed a certain notoriety from its involvement in the Palm Sunday rally and shortly thereafter led a student walkout at the Burbank High School in San Antonio. This action in San Antonio prompted the school board to change its high school curriculum to answer the needs of Mexican American students.

In June, 1969, MAYO, which had been funded by the Ford Foundation, was ordered to desist in its political activities or suffer the loss of funding. The Ford Foundation had recently been under attack from Congress for financing seemingly political organizations. In a decision which threatened to destroy the fledgling organization, MAYO's new chairman, Mario Compean, recommended immediate separation from the foundation. Six months later, in December, the now-unfunded MAYO launched its Winter Garden Project.

The purpose of the Winter Garden Project was to interest

[47]Lamb, *Sons of the Southwest*, p. 123.

Chicano youth in politics. Its stated purpose was to demand that a ten-county area in southern Texas be set aside for Chicanos, but more importantly, it was an attempt to incite Chicano self-determinism. A similar project had been instituted in Crystal City, Texas, with surprising success, and MAYO leaders hoped to apply the ingredients of this success throughout all of southern Texas.[48]

Presently, MAYO is growing. Its appeal is largely to Chicano youth, especially at the college level, where several branches of the organization now exist.

THE MEXICAN AMERICAN POLITICAL ASSOCIATION

The Chicano has always faced political and economic inequality in the United States. Following World War II, a group of political activists headed by Bert Corona and Edward Quevedo decided to do something about it. Calling a meeting in Fresno, California, in April of 1960, Corona and 150 volunteer delegates formed the Mexican American Political Association (MAPA). Its major objectives were to:

1. encourage Mexican Americans to become actively involved in political parties;
2. get Mexican Americans out in voter registration drives;
3. use Mexican American voter strength as a wedge to force candidate and issue response to the needs of Chicanos; and
4. gain cultural, social, economic, and civic improvements for Mexican Americans.

MAPA demonstrated its strength in the 1962 elections when, thanks to Mexican American bloc voting, Edward Roybal went to the U.S. House of Representatives, the first Mexican American in the federal legislature. The organization also managed to elect a Chicano to the lower house of the California legislature.

In recent years, MAPA has become increasingly involved in the area of civil rights and discrimination.

THE LEAGUE OF UNITED LATIN AMERICAN CITIZENS

America in the twenties was a time of hip-flasks, free-wheeling, and unprecedented prosperity. The stock market soared

---

[48]Rendon, *Chicano Manifesto,* pp. 197-203.

and the mood of the nation was one of optimism. But America in the twenties was also a time of the Ku Klux Klan, of the Sacco-Vanzetti trial, of the numerous red scares—a time of paranoia. In Texas this paranoia manifested itself in acts of racism against Mexican Americans. KKK activity increased greatly, and even the famed Texas Rangers seemed inclined to protect Anglo interests at the expense of Mexican Americans. As a result of this discrimination, and in opposition to the second-class citizenship of Mexican Americans, the League of United Latin American Citizens (LULAC) formed in San Antonio, Texas, on February 17, 1929.

An outgrowth of the order Sons of America in San Antonio, LULAC adopted policies promoting patriotism and the "Americanization" of Mexican Americans to counter racism. Section I of LULAC's constitution states: "As loyal citizens of the United States of America: We believe in the democratic principle of individual political and religious freedom."[49] The constitution further outlines the organization's goals as gaining access to the professions, improving education, encouraging the learning of English, promoting active political participation, eliminating racism, developing self-pride, and achieving equality.

In the more than four decades of LULAC's existence, it has been notably active in the field of education. In 1931 it won an important desegregation case against the Texas State Board of Education. This success was repeated in a 1945-47 case against the school system of Orange County, California. In the area of employment, LULAC pressured the legislature of New Mexico into adopting a policy against job discrimination in 1949. During the sixties, the organization was active in suits against the exploitation of migrant labor and against discriminatory practices in jury selection, poll taxes, and the *bracero* program.

Boasting a membership of 100,000, LULAC works today for the recognition of the needs of agricultural workers, aid for migrant workers, and the use of bilingual programs in schools with Mexican American children. This involves operating as a pressure group on the local, state, and federal government.

[49]Steiner, *La Raza,* p. 181.

LA RAZA UNIDA

El Partido de La Raza Unida was established in Crystal City, Texas, in January, 1970. An outgrowth of the notion that Chicanos would never be able to control their own destinies under the existing two-party political system, *La Raza Unida* sprang forth under the guiding hand of José Angel Gutierrez, who had been one of the creators of MAYO. In establishing this new, independent Chicano political party, Gutierrez used the old, time-proven philosophy urged by Saul Alinsky: equality cannot exist unless both sides of the issue have power.[50]

The center of *La Raza Unida*—which has now spread into twenty Texas counties and a number of other states—is Crystal City. From there, the "Spinach Capital of America," *La Raza Unida* promotes the principle of Chicano involvement in the control of institutions which affect Mexican Americans. The example set in Crystal City shows just how Chicanos can gain control. Following a program of voter education and registration, *La Raza Unida* candidates overwhelmingly unseated the Anglo power bloc in the 1970 school board elections. Operating from this power base, the newly elected candidates began instituting reforms to make the schools more responsive to Chicano needs. From this, they used their influence to affect other institutions.

From its start in southern Texas, *La Raza Unida Party* has become a symbol of Chicano self-determination. Branches have opened in several states, including Arizona, New Mexico, California, Colorado, and Michigan, which aim at overcoming political apathy and instituting needed reforms. Perhaps its chief accomplishment, however, has been the creation of a new sense of pride and unity among Mexican Americans and other Spanish-speaking people in the United States.

[50]Meier and Rivera, *The Chicanos*, p. 276.

10

THE MEXICAN AMERICAN EXPERIENCE

THE BORDERLANDS—INITIAL EXPLORATION

THE NEW WORLD stretched out before the Spanish conquista-dores, a seemingly endless land of jungles, deserts, mountains, valleys, and plains—and a land holding out the promise of immeasurable wealth. The Aztecs had been conquered, their temples plundered for gold and their population decimated by the ravages of disease and war. The mighty Incas of Peru had fallen to the treachery of Francisco Pizarro. Throughout regions ranging from southern Chile all the way to Florida, relentless explorers searched basins and valleys seeking yet another civili-zation to offer its wealth to the Spanish empire. In 1536, a year after the Spanish province of Mexico had received its first viceroy, a lost conquistador stumbled into Mexico City with the tale of fabulous wealth to the north.

Cabeza de Vaca had spent eight years among the Indian tribes of Texas and northern Mexico. A survivor of an ill-fated expedition to Florida, he had learned survival by adopting the Indian ways, and from the Indians he had heard fantastic stories of the Seven Cities of Cíbola, the legendary cities of gold supposedly founded by seven Portuguese bishops who had fled their homeland.

Great excitement was generated by De Vaca's news, and Viceroy Antonio de Mendoza quickly dispatched a small expe-dition northward to investigate De Vaca's claim. Consisting of Fray Marcos de Niza, of the order of St. Francis, Estebanico (the "Black Mexican"), and a party of Indians, the expedition explored parts of New Mexico and Arizona, but failed to locate the golden cities. Yet, when Fray Marcos returned to the capital three years later (Estebanico had been killed by Zuñi Indians) he claimed to have actually seen the cities. Speculation and gossip abounded in the capital and another expedition was assembled.

The following year, six hundred Spaniards and Indians accompanied Francisco Vásquez de Coronado on his monumental trek into Arizona, New Mexico, Texas, and Kansas. Early in the expedition, Coronado discovered the obvious—the cities of gold were merely Indian villages. He punished the Indians at Cíbola by killing several of their number and pushed on into the buffalo country, seeking Quivira, the city of gold and wealth on the Great Plains. But the Golden Quivira turned out to be another collection of Indian villages, and Coronado, discouraged and possessing no more wealth than he had started with, turned his expedition southward and marched back to Mexico City.

Meanwhile, Juan Rodríguez Cabrillo had taken two ships to explore the western coast of the continent. On September 25, 1542, he discovered the Bay of San Diego. Sailing northwards, he dropped anchor at various points and went ashore to meet with Indians inhabiting the coastal regions of California. From these tribal representatives he learned of other Spaniards east of the great wall of mountains (probably the Coronado expedition). Continuing his coastal expedition, Cabrillo reached a point somewhere around the San Francisco Bay area. Here, having failed to find the great stores of wealth the Spanish sought, he turned his ships homeward. For the next fifty years the lands to the north of Mexico, which were destined to become the borderlands of the United States and the residence of millions of Mexican Americans, remained virtually untouched, the home of the native Indian populations which inhabited them.

JUAN DE OÑATE

Juan de Oñate had made a fortune in the silver mines at Zacatecas. In 1598, after receiving a royal charter to explore, settle, and develop new lands north of Mexico, Oñate set out with an expedition of four hundred people and seven thousand head of cattle. From the site of El Paso the party moved up the Rio Grande, and on April 30 it took possession of the territory of New Mexico in the name of the Spanish king. San Juan de los Caballeros, the first Spanish settlement in New Mexico, was established in the Chama River valley, and Oñate assumed the duties of provisional governor. In 1608 he was removed from his post. The following year his successor established Sante Fe, which became the capital of the province. By 1630 the initial expedition had founded twenty-five missions, with a string of settlements from Texas to Arizona. As noble as the enterprise was, these early outposts proved to be temporary. In 1680 the Pueblo Indians, led by Popé revolted and drove the Spanish settlers from New Mexico. Churches were destroyed, *villas* burned, and several hundred settlers killed in the uprising. Twelve years elapsed before the Spaniards were able to reconquer the province and reestablish the settlements.

FATHER KINO

Until the latter part of the seventeenth century the region which later became Arizona remained an unappetizingly arid and hostile province. Included in the Spanish empire as part of Juan de Oñate's territorial claim in 1598 were portions of Arizona, charted by a few exploratory expeditions. Fray Marcos de Niza had included it in his search for the seven cities of gold, as had Coronado, but the intractable character of the land and fierce Indian resistance discouraged any ideas about settlement. In 1687, however, a Jesuit missionary, explorer, and cartographer devoted the last twenty-four years of his life to converting the Indians of southern Arizona and northern Sonora.

Father Eusebio Francisco Kino, an Italian by birth, chose to live among the Pima Indians of northern Sonora. He carried Christianity and the Spanish culture to natives inhabiting the lands from California to New Mexico. He called this region Pimería Alta, and he baptized hundreds of Indians. In 1700 he founded the mission of San Xavier del Bac near modern Tucson, which remains a monument to the Spanish era. In addition to his missionary work, Father Kino conducted approximately forty journeys of· exploration throughout the Southwest. He charted the Colorado from the mouth of the Gila to the Gulf of

California, and his many maps of the region became famous for their accuracy, especially his 1705 map, "A Land Passage to California." Through his honesty and brave example he helped open the Arizona territory for colonization.

FRAY JUNIPERO SERRA

The coast of California had been explored several times throughout the sixteenth and early seventeenth centuries. Hernando de Alarcon explored the Gulf of California in 1540; the following year, Francisco de Ulloa supposedly named the region *California* after a mythical country in a Spanish romantic novel; Juan Rodriguez Cabrillo explored the Santa Barbara Islands and the coast in 1542, sailing north to the San Francisco Bay area; Sir Francis Drake, the English navigator, sailed along the coast in 1579; and Sebastian Vizcaino entered the San Diego and Monterey bays in 1602-03. By 1700 missionaries had established settlements in Lower California, but the regions north of the Baja Peninsula remained uncolonized. In 1769, however, Russian settlers began spreading into northern California, and the Spanish colonial government ordered the immediate colonization of Upper California. The task of coordinating this colonization effort fell to Fray Junipero Serra, a Franciscan missionary.

Father Serra, born on an island off Spain, had been in Mexico for twenty years, since 1749, before his assignment to open the territory of northern California came. Though sick and partially crippled, he undertook his task with great zeal and by mid-summer had founded the mission at San Diego. The following year, the mission at Monterey was established. Three years later he returned to Mexico City to help organize the overland expedition of Juan Bautista de Anza to explore and open the territory to San Francisco. By 1823, largely through Father Serra's efforts, a string of twenty-one missions stretched from San Diego to San Francisco.

FRONTIER INSTITUTIONS

Spain was the first European colonial power to come to the New World and to that portion of the United States now

designated the Southwest. Driven by the dual purpose of acquir-
ing wealth and spreading Christianity, the conquistadores, missionaries, and early settlers embarked upon a difficult and
hazardous crusade to transform the land and culture of the
Indian inhabitants. The ultimate goal, of course, was to create
"civilized" Spanish-oriented settlements which would expand
the Spanish empire and supply a constant flow of wealth to
Madrid.

The early explorers ventured into the borderlands, mapping
its regions and seeking other civilizations to parallel that of the
Aztecs and Incas. This initial exploration accomplished, small
groups of missionaries and settlers moved northward to begin
the grueling work of establishing secured outposts in a hostile
and deadly environment. The failure of the Oñate settlements in
1680 led Spanish authorities to adopt new tactics in future
colonial enterprises. Thus came the development of the frontier
institutions of the *presidio,* the mission, and the *pueblo.*

The *presidio* was an army post, fortified and quartering as
many as a hundred soldiers. Usually built near missions or
civilian settlements, its primary purpose was protection. During
an emergency such as an Indian raid, soldiers could be quickly
dispatched to the trouble spot, or if the situation warranted,
colonials could be gathered inside.

As the *presidio* operated as the institution for protection,
the mission existed to civilize the indigenous population.
Authorized and financed in part by the government, missions
gathered numbers of Indians into their sphere of influence and
taught them the skills, attitudes, and religion of their Spanish
conquerors. After the Indian had been sufficiently civilized,
that is, converted into a model Spanish American, he was released
from the mission confines and sent out to convince other
Indians to adopt the Spanish ways. Thus, when a given area had
been pacified with the majority of Indians residing in peaceful,
Spanish-dominated towns and villages, the mission ceased functioning as a frontier institution and became a parish church.

The *pueblo* complemented the *presidio* and mission by
acting as the civilian counterpart to these military and religious
institutions. Designed for permanence after the other two had
fulfilled their purpose, the *pueblo* operated according to well-
defined laws governing such things as street and plaza size,

revenue lands, land for private use, the *ejido* (lands held for common use), and the *suerte* (land having access to water). The *pueblo* system was created with interests of both the individual and the municipality in mind. Consequently, many of its legal foundations, especially those relating to water rights, exist today.

ANGLO-AMERICAN IMMIGRATION

Beginning in the early nineteenth century, Anglo-Americans began immigrating to the Southwest. This immigration started slowly, a mere trickle in comparison to the hoards which would come later, and Spain—and after the Mexican Revolution, the early independent government in Mexico City—did not consider them a threat at first. Throughout the borderland provinces the handful of American settlers received grants of land in exchange for accepting Mexican citizenship and joining, or at least professing to join, the Roman Catholic Church. In Texas, however, American immigration led to Mexican-Anglo hostility which surfaced almost immediately.

In 1821, Moses Austin received a grant from the Mexican government to settle three hundred families in Texas. Although he died before his colonizing plan began, his son Stephen took over the project and the following year settled the "original three hundred" on the banks of the Colorado River. All went well for a time, but by 1830 enough friction had developed for Mexico to ban further immigration from the United States. The Texans ignored this ban and another which prohibited slavery. They distrusted the unstable Mexican government and disregarded Mexican customs. Already, talk of independence flourished throughout the Texas province.

When Santa Anna assumed the presidency of Mexico in 1833, the revolutionary fervor subsided briefly. The Texans felt that this self-proclaimed reformer would allow them the degree of autonomy they sought, which included granting Texas statehood in the Republic of Mexico. But Santa Anna had no such intentions and after three years of warnings and anti-Texan rhetoric led an army into the province to enforce obedience to Mexican laws. The Mexican army stormed San Antonio, defeating a group of Texans at the Alamo. From there, Santa Anna attacked Goliad, ordering the execution of all Texas prisoners.

In the midst of this confusion, Texas declared independence, and on April 21, forces under Sam Houston attacked the Mexican army at the San Jacinto River. Santa Anna was taken prisoner and readily signed the treaty recognizing Texas' independence.

The Texas revolution, the outcome of Anglo-American settlement in northern Coahuila, set the stage for two bitter conflicts. It precipitated a war between Mexico and the United States, and it embittered Anglos, especially in Texas, towards the Mexican people. Racial hostility, fueled by the defeat and subsequent execution of Texans at the Alamo and at Goliad, created attitudes and prejudices which persist even today. In the period following the revolution, these racial antagonisms frequently flared into violence. Texans raided Mexican settlements and Mexicans retaliated. In the section of land between the Nueces and Rio Grande rivers, virtual warfare existed for nearly a decade, until the Treaty of Guadalupe Hidalgo set the border along the Rio Grande; and even then, guerrillas, bandits, posses, citizens groups, and the Texas Rangers kept that stretch of territory in southern Texas a no-man's land of bloodshed and terror.

THE AFTERMATH OF THE MEXICAN-AMERICAN WAR

The Treaty of Guadalupe Hidalgo (1848) which ended the war between Mexico and the United States set the Texas boundary at the Rio Grande and ceded New Mexico, Arizona, and California to the United States. Mexico was compensated $15 million for its lost territory and received guarantees that the Mexican citizens residing in the affected provinces would retain their property rights as well as their cultural rights to use the Spanish language, practice Catholicism, and adhere to their previous customs. After a period of one year, those residents electing to remain in the United States would become U.S. citizens, subject to its laws and recipient of its basic rights. As fair as these guarantees seemed on paper, however, in reality they were quickly forgotten.

The discovery of gold at Sutter's Mill in northern California lured great numbers of Anglo-Americans westward. Overnight,

California was transformed from a pastoral, Spanish-speaking province to a bustling maze of mining towns. English quickly replaced Spanish as the dominant language, and quiet *pueblos* became sprawling cities complete with gamblers, gunslingers, and greedy prospectors. For a time Hispano ranchers in southern California enjoyed great prosperity supplying cattle to the gold fields. But the introduction of superior beef cattle from the Great Plains broke their market, leading to the breakup of their huge grants. For the average Mexican, sadly, the gold rush meant a worse fate.

The first Anglo-Americans to reach the gold fields were a tough and often unscrupulous lot. They harbored prejudices, amplified by the Mexican-American War, against anything or anyone Mexican and did not hesitate to vent their anger. Mexicans were lynched and murdered, their lands and personal property stolen. In Sonora, two years after the Mexican-American War had ended, an American mob of two thousand miners burned a Mexican camp and killed scores of Mexican miners. This action followed the passage of a foreign-miners' tax in the California legislature to end competition from Mexican miners. Other lynchings took place and violence against Mexicans and Mexican Americans continued unchecked, forcing large numbers of the original settlers' ancestors to seek refuge in the Baja Peninsula and northern Mexico. An immediate outcome of this persecution was the formation of Mexican guerrilla bands to protect Mexican rights and take revenge for the injustices dealt them. The most famous of these "Mexican bandits" was Joaquín Murrieta, who boasted an army of two thousand men and conducted lightning raids which terrorized much of California during this period.

In Texas, where hostility and contempt for all things Mexican had been deeply ingrained since the Texas Revolution, violence reached frightening proportions. The Texas Rangers became the official agency of law and order and the unofficial agency of Anglo-American supremacy. Vigilante groups and secret organizations terrorized the Mexican American population, often using Mexican opposition to slavery as justification for their actions. An example of this occurred in 1856 when Mexican Americans were ordered to vacate two Texas counties after a proposed Negro insurrection was uncovered. The Texans believed that the resident Mexican Americans were responsible for this plot. In other counties this incident led to the passage of discriminatory bills including recommendations against the hiring of Mexican laborers and forbidding travel without passes. As this anti-Mexican fervor spread, an outbreak of raids along the Texas border culminated in the infamous "Cortina War."

The Cortina War began in 1859 when Juan Cortina, the "red robber of the Rio Grande," freed a family servant from a Texas jail. For the next thirteen years Cortina and his band raided Anglo settlements in the borderland. Texans, unable to capture the elusive Cortina, retaliated by raiding and burning the homes of Mexicans suspected of sympathizing with the outlaw band. Cortina was captured in 1783, but the period of lawlessness did not cease. The continuing raids of Mexican *banditti* led to indiscriminate and brutal reprisals against Mexican American settlements.

Aside from the violence in both California and Texas which set the pattern for later relations between Mexican Americans and Anglo-Americans, the period following the Mexican-American War also was characterized by the transfer of great tracts of land from the conquered to the conqueror. When the Americans arrived in the Southwest, they found most of the land taken, assigned by Spanish and Mexican land grants. What followed, then, was an era of legal and quasi-legal chicanery, fraud, and theft in which Anglo-American interests gradually gained control of most of these lands. Ultimately, two systems of property ownership clashed, and although not all lands were thus exchanged, the systems and legalities of the conqueror prevailed.

The aftermath of the Mexican-American War rendered the former masters of the Southwest impotent, relegating them to the status of a minority group with the characteristic implications of second-class citizenship. Discrimination and violence and certainly exploitation emerged as the legacy of the ancestors of the Spanish conquistadores.

THE GREAT MIGRATION

To many Mexicans the territory of the United States bordering on Mexico has always really been a part of Mexico. The lay of the land is the same; the ancestral ties are present; and relatives and friends reside there. The Indian owned it first; then the Spaniard, followed by the Republic of Mexico; and presently it is part of the territory claimed by the United States. But perhaps that too is only temporary. *Quien sabe?* Mexicans have always traveled back and forth quite freely, crossing and recrossing a boundary existing more on paper, in the words and agreements of politicians, and in the minds of the Border Patrol than in actual geography. Thus, immigration has been relatively free of the trauma faced by the European immigrant. As an immigration group, the great waves of Mexican nationals seeking job security and freedom from political and economic turmoil arrived late in the saga of U.S. immigration. They came after the peak of European immigration. And unlike the European immigrant, many returned, for a large number of Mexicans came with the intention of one day returning to their homeland. In the twentieth century there have been three great waves of immigration from Mexico. The first began in 1910 as the Mexican Revolution spurred thousands of refugees to leave the chaos at home in favor of at least some security in the United States. The second occurred during the twenties as the political and economic instability of post-revolution Mexico and the new prosperity of the American Southwest pushed and pulled even more Mexicans northward. The third wave was initiated by the Second World War, as Mexican agricultural workers ventured into the Southwest lured by the demand for farm labor.

During the decade of 1910 to 1920, well over 200,000 immigrants left Mexico for the United States as the Mexican Revolution sent great numbers of political refugees and displaced persons northward. For the most part, the political refugees were educated and accustomed to aristocratic living, and as such they integrated easily into the Anglo society. The displaced persons, however—by far the majority—possessed few skills and did not have the educational background of the *gente de razón*. Often crossing the border with little more than the clothes on their back, these economic and social refugees had been caught in the uproar of political change and wanted little more than to scratch out a living. They had fled to the United States with that hope in mind, and in the United States discovered that they had one commodity in demand—their labor.

The United States had recently curtailed Chinese and Japanese immigration (through the Chinese Exclusion Act of 1882 and the Gentlemen's Agreement with Japan in 1907), which had supplied the bulk of cheap labor in the Southwest. In addition, this first wave coincided with a period in American history in which droves of Anglo-Americans were abandoning the rural in favor of the urban life. Scores of former producers of agricultural products were now consumers, and agricultural interests, especially in the Southwest, expanded to meet this booming new market. All this required labor. And if the grower was to make a profit, it required cheap labor. In the midst of this growth, World War I erupted, worsening the labor shortage as Anglo manpower was drawn into the armed forces. Special regulations were effected to recruit labor from Mexico to augment the flow of immigrants, and job opportunities opened in areas other than agriculture.

The second great wave of Mexican immigration, from 1920 to 1930, occurred as a result of two major pressures: political and economic instability in .post-revolution Mexico, and the attraction of a new period of prosperity in the Southwest. Although accurate figures are difficult to arrive at, estimates set this second wave at nearly a half million Mexicans who gathered their meager belongings and moved north.

Post-revolution Mexico remained in a state of confusion. The Porfirio Diaz regime had been overthrown, and a succession of presidents attempted to restore order and initiate the agrarian and other reforms the revolution had called for. A new Mexican constitution drafted in 1917 had committed the nation to public welfare, but so far the machinery of the new governments, crippled by political intrigue and exhausted resources, failed to respond to the needs of the masses.

In the United States the era of prosperity following World War I offered at least the opportunity to make a living. The agricultural growth which had begun the previous decade continued. Improved irrigation and food market technology, such as refrigerated boxcars and key advances in the canning industry, stimulated the trend towards large-scale farming. All this required labor. But Mexican labor was not confined to the infant agri-business interests. Railroads, both construction and maintenance, mining, and manufacturing drew heavily from

Mexican immigration as a source of low-wage labor. In turn, Mexicans readily fit into these industries, in many cases the same industries their ancestors had helped develop, and their contributions bolstered the economic growth of the Southwest.

By 1930 over a million Mexicans had immigrated to the United States. They constituted the majority of the work force in agriculture, mining, and the Western railroads. For the most part they settled in the old Spanish borderlands, the fan of settlement south of a line drawn from Los Angeles to El Paso. They had been welcomed, recruited, and allowed to cross relatively unhindered into the Southwest—but then the Great Depression struck.

The Depression halted the free flow of Mexican immigration. Agriculture was in trouble, as were other businesses, and the hiring of Mexicans as a source of cheap labor gave way to the hiring of unemployed Anglos. As the Dust Bowl crisis drove thousands of "Okies" westward and factories and small businesses shut down, the labor market was flooded. Federal authorities enforced strict immigration controls and people of Mexican descent were encouraged to return to their native land. Many went voluntarily, but tens of thousands were compelled to return to Mexico as part of a massive repatriation program.

The outbreak of World War II again opened the labor market in the Southwest. This time, however, increasing prosperity in Mexico also placed a demand on labor. To offset its shortages, the United States negotiated with Mexico for the use of temporary agricultural workers. This led to the *bracero* program in which the United States acted as a labor contractor for American agricultural interests. The program lasted until 1964, and many *braceros* later returned on permanent visas. Another facet of this era was the entrance of large numbers of illegal immigrants, the so-called "wetbacks."

There have always been "wetbacks" in the Southwest, but during World War II their numbers increased significantly. Many American growers readily employed illegals, thus avoiding the red tape and fees involved in the *bracero* program, and the "wetback" problem was soon out of control. For every agricultural worker admitted legally, four illegals were apprehended by the Border Patrol. Beginning in 1954, the U.S. Immigration and Nationalization Service instituted "Operation Wetback" to halt this flow and return these illegals, whose presence generally depressed wages and conditions for domestic workers.

Permanent immigration continued at a high rate during the fifties. Nearly 300,000 Mexicans attracted by the farm labor market entered the United States. In 1965, amendments to the Immigration and Nationality Act fixed a quota of 120,000 per year for Mexican immigration.

Although Mexican immigration continues, the great floods of people crossing the border, an estimated ten percent of Mexico's population, have subsided. Growing prosperity and reform in Mexico have been able to slow the rate of those leaving. Those who came, however, have provided a significant contribution to the growth of the Southwest. Vital transportation provided by Western railroads and the agricultural industry so vital to the nation's well-being have been the largest beneficiaries of their labor. As the Southwest continues to expand, immigration will undoubtedly continue to supply a sizable portion of the labor required.

PART THREE
RED POWER:

THE AMERICAN INDIAN

11

RED POWER

THE NEW INDIANS

ON NOVEMBER 20, 1969, some eighty Indians calling themselves Indians of All Tribes invaded Alcatraz Island, the twelve acre former prison in San Francisco Bay. Hoping to dramatize the plight of the American Indians, the members of All Tribes claimed the island under an old Sioux treaty stipulating that unused federal land (Alcatraz was closed in 1963) would revert to the Indians. "There's a lot of symbolism in us taking Alcatraz, the prison," commented John Trudell, one of the leaders of the occupation. "We Indian people, we've been prisoners in our own land."[1] Intent upon establishing an Indian cultural center, the All Tribes Council offered to placate angry federal authorities by purchasing the island for "$24 worth of glass beads and red cloth." The Alcatraz Indians were expelled by federal marshals a year and a half later, but the expulsion did little to quell the rising rebellion among the nation's 800,000 Indians.

Since the mid-sixties, frustration with economic and social conditions besetting Indians and a deep impatience with the federal bureaucracy, which according to one militant "has ministered to the Indian poeple like a colonial power," have bred an era of Indian activism. In the state of Washington, Indians have

---

[1] "Alcatraz Island Becomes Indian Freedom Symbol," *The Grand Rapids Press*, March 29, 1970, p. 3A.

held Fish-Ins protesting the state's fishing regulations, which violate their treaty rights. Along the Pacific Coast, the Quinault Indians closed down a twenty-nine-mile stretch of beach to prevent white vacationers from further littering their land. In Maine, Indians of the Passamaquoddy Tribe formed a human barrier across U.S. 1 and charged travelers a dollar per car to pass. And on cars across the nation bumper stickers proclaimed: RED POWER! INDIAN POWER! CUSTER HAD IT COMING! STOP THE WAR ON INDIANS! and KEMO SABE MEANS HONKY!

In recent years, a segment of Indians have pushed for more dramatic demonstrations. In November, 1972, a caravan of approximately 500 Indian men, women, and children descended upon Washington, D.C., protesting the nearly 400 treaty agreements which the federal government has failed, either in part or in whole, to fulfill. Spurred by the militant American Indian Movement (AIM), the demonstrators occupied the Bureau of Indian Affairs building and, tongue-in-cheek, renamed it "The Native American Embassy." After a week of occupation and an estimated $2.28 million in damage, the protesters left, having received promises that the Administration would study their grievances.

Within four months, AIM had opened another offensive to keep national and international attention focused on the Indian movement. This time, March, 1973, they moved onto the Oglala Sioux Pine Ridge Reservation in South Dakota and occupied the tiny settlement of Wounded Knee, site of the infamous massacre of 200 Indians by the U.S. Cavalry in 1890. As the initial invasion stretched into weeks of armed occupation, public attention waxed and then waned, but AIM's demands were heard. In essence they were asking for (1) a Congressional investigation of the Bureau of Indian Affairs; (2) recognition of the 1868 Fort Laramie Treaty; (3) a foreign relations committee to investigate the nearly 400 broken treaties; and (4) recognition of the Sioux and other tribes as sovereign nations. "We have exhausted our diplomatic efforts," said Vernon Bellacourt, National Field Director for AIM, "that's the reason for Wounded Knee."[2]

[2]"The Dick Cavett Show," March, 1973. Vernon Bellacourt, Robert

The poorest of the poor, Indians suffer the highest unemployment, birth, infant mortality, suicide, and alcoholism rates in the nation. They also are the poorest educated, have the lowest incomes, and have the shortest life expectancy of any group in America. To the Indian many of these conditions are attributable to the Bureau of Indian Affairs—frequently called the Colonial Office—which acts as a paternalistic, all-encompassing body, an occasionally corrupt, often incompetent white man's bureaucracy. At times seeming like a red-tape octopus, the BIA covers practically every phase of Indian life. It educates him, feeds him, holds his land in trust, and is answerable not to him but to Congress, which itself has not always acted in the best interest of Indians. Yet the Indian is not ready to give up the BIA—it is all he has.

Red Power leaders see as an alternative to the federal government's mismanagement of Indian affairs the policy of self-determination: Indian control of Indian affairs. In the past, the government has ministered to Indians as "wards" and not, as stipulated in the treaties, as a sovereign nation entering into agreement with another sovereign nation. Indians today are saying, in the words of Vernon Bellacourt, "We must be dealt with as a sovereign people."[3] Although not all Indians agree with Bellacourt's stand, they at least agree with Robert Burnette, leader of the American Indian Civil Rights Council, when he says, "Give us a chance to control our own destiny."[4]

This new concern for self-determination is taking various directions. In education, tribes have begun instituting their own schools employing Indian teachers and including Indian history and the Indian heritage in their studies. In business, Indians are working towards tribally owned and operated ventures to help bolster reservation economies as well as trying to attract private industry to the reservations. In the courts, tribes are determined to carry on battles for civil, land, and water rights which are

---

Burnette of the American Indian Civil Rights Council, and the three traditional chiefs of the Oglala Sioux appeared on this talk show in order to present their side of the Wounded Knee issue.

[3] *Ibid.*
[4] *Ibid.*

legally theirs. In other areas, Indians are demanding recognition for disregarded treaties, are pressing for the extension of federal services to urban Indians, are demanding protection from state and local governments, and are determined to secure the right to live as they see fit.

Although the Red Power Movement suffers several handicaps, the most important being the fractionalization of the 467 tribal bodies in the United States, including Alaska, it is making gains. The occupations of Alcatraz and Wounded Knee have focused public attention on Indian conditions. In recent years the courts have followed a trend of awarding cases in the favor of Indians. As a result, Indian fishing rights in Washington and Michigan have been upheld; the Taos Pueblo of New Mexico recently received back 48,000 acres which had been illegally included as part of the Kit Carson National Forest; nearly $500 million have so far been paid in reparation to various tribes for lands taken; and, perhaps the most significant of changes, government officials have wavered from their hard line on assimilation.

For the past hundred years the federal government, and various church groups, have encouraged Indians to abandon the Indian life and take up the life and society of the white man. Indians, however, have balked at this idea. As Vine Deloria, Jr., perhaps the most widely respected Indian spokesman, has said, "It just seems to a lot of Indians that this continent was a lot better off when we were running it." Consequently, Indians have held out against white pressure to assimilate. "You just don't throw away thousands of years of cultural tradition," said one Sioux leader.

After a hundred years of failure, the government seems at least willing to listen to the Indian. As former President Nixon said in 1970: "We must recognize that American society can allow many different cultures to flourish in harmony, and we must provide an opportunity for those Indians wishing to do so to lead a useful and prosperous life in an Indian environment."[5] Whether the government will continue to listen is unknown, but one thing that can be virtually assured is that Red Power leaders will not stop talking, or acting, to create an American Indian

[5]Gary Blonston, "The Indian Troubles of '73," *Detroit Free Press*, April 8, 1973, p. 4D.

dream—to be an Indian and not be penalized by the currently dominant society.

RED POWER DEFINED

Red Power is the concept of self-determination whereby Indians cast off their dependent role and assert their right to control their own destiny and live as they see fit. As Vine Deloria, Jr., said at a 1966 convention of the National Congress of American Indians: "Red Power means we want power over our own lives. We do not wish to threaten anyone. We do not wish power over anyone. . . . We simply want the power, the political and economic power, to run our own lives in our own way."[6] Ernie Stevens, chairman of the California Inter-Tribal Council, put it more simply: "Red Power—it means that we Indians want to do things for ourselves."[7]

Red Power as a movement had its birth during the sixties as young, college-educated Indians—"Red Muslims"—watched with increasing frustration the gains made by other minorities during the Civil Rights Movement. Self-determination as a concept was not new, but in practice it needed a catalyst. Indian problems differed basically from black problems. Both groups suffered poverty and discrimination, but where blacks were victims of neglect, Indians were victims of paternalism; where blacks were victims of cultural exclusion, Indians were victims of intensive pressure for assimilation; and where blacks had no land base nor treaty guarantees, Indians had these, though they were constantly imperiled. The catalyst for Red Power came when so-called "black extremists" began speaking in terms of Black Nationalism, the concept of black self-determination which formed the basis for the Black Power philosophy. "Black Power, as a communications phenomenon, was a godsend to other groups," commented Vine Deloria, Jr., in *Custer Died for Your Sins: An Indian Manifesto*. "It clarified the intellectual concepts which had kept Indians and Mexicans confused and allowed the concept of self-determination suddenly to become valid."[8]

[6]Stan Steiner, *The New Indians* (New York: Delta Books, 1968), p. 269.
[7]"Red Power," *Grand Rapids Press*, January 11, 1970, p. 3A.
[8]Vine Deloria, Jr., *Custer Died for Your Sins: An Indian Manifesto* (New York: Avon, 1969), pp. 181-182.

For the Indians, self-determination includes self-government, control of Indian lands and resources, and the right to determine programs and policies for Indians. Central to these rights is the maintenance of treaty obligations by the federal government. Treaties between the tribes and the United States were made, both legally and morally, between sovereign nations. They are contracts setting boundaries and providing certain guarantees and compensations for lands taken. As such, Red Power advocates insist, as Alvin M. Josephy, Jr., explains, "on the inviolability of their land and on the strict observance and protection of obligations and rights guaranteed the Indians by treaties with the federal government."[9]

In essence, Red Power asks Indians to look at themselves, take pride in their cultural heritage, adapt modern society to their modern Indianness, and assert themselves and their Indianness. On December 16, 1969, the Indians occupying Alcatraz sent a letter to all the Indians of North America. In it they said, "We feel that the only reason Indian people have been able to hold on and survive through decades of persecution and cultural deprivation is that the Indian way of life is and has been strong enough to hold the people together."[10] In a call for unity, pride, and self-determination which forms the foundation of Red Power, the Indians of Alcatraz recognized the importance of Indian values and strengths and of the Indian way of life as a viable alternative to the increasing complexity and turmoil of twentieth-century America. They issued an appeal for all Indians to join them, explaining: "We realize . . . that we are not getting anywhere fast by working alone as individual tribes. If we can gather together as brothers and come to a common agreement, we feel that we can be much more effective, doing things for ourselves, instead of having someone else doing it, telling us what is good for us."

EDUCATION

Almost from the beginning of white-Indian relations the white man has seen fit to usurp the Indian's traditional pro-

[9]Alvin M. Josephy, Jr., ed., *Red Power: The American Indians Fight for Freedom* (Scarborough, Ont.: McGraw-Hill Ryerson, 1971), p. 5.

[10]*Ibid.*, p. 188, citing a letter sent to Indians of all tribes in North America, December 16, 1969.

cesses of education. In place of the tradition of knowledge being passed down by village elders, parents, and uncles, the white man constructed schools. The ultimate goal has been to refashion Indian youth, making them cultural and social replicas of white civilization able to be assimilated into the mainstream society. The results have been dismal failure. Of all the minority groups in the United States today, the American Indian remains the least educated. Sadly, this tragedy is compounded, for in being forced to seek the white man's knowledge, the Indian student has also been forced to sacrifice his tribal knowledge and cultural heritage. It remained for a new generation of Indians to realize that white-administered and white-dominated education did not answer Indian needs. Self-determination was the key to achieving quality Indian education.

In 1973 about 200,000 Indian students between the ages of five and eighteen were enrolled in school. Nearly two-thirds attended public schools, a fourth attended schools operated by the federal government, and roughly five percent were enrolled in mission schools.[11] Originally, various church groups had established mission schools to educate and Christianize the American Indian. As early as 1568, the Jesuits had created a school for the children of dispossessed Florida Indians. Gradually, however, as the United States grew in stature and size, it assumed the responsibility for Indian education. Through a number of separate treaties, one of the first being with members of the Iroquois Nation in 1794, the government found itself promising to teach Indian children to read and write.

At first, it fulfilled this obligation by funding mission groups, and it was not until 1860 that the first non-mission federal Indian school was started. From that point, prompted by Congressional pressure, the government stopped funding mission groups and began operating its own schools through the Bureau of Indian Affairs. By 1971 there were more than 200 federally run Indian schools in existence, plus nineteen dormitories for Indians in public schools. The enrollment in BIA schools and dormitories was approximately 57,000 in 1972. In

[11]Figures for 1973 released by the United States Department of the Interior in "Statistics Concerning Indian Education." The figures were rounded for easier reading. Those interested in current statistics can write to the Department of the Interior.

public schools that number was more than doubled, with an enrollment of 130,000.[12] Yet, despite treaty obligations, and despite the availability of these federal, public, and mission school facilities, the government has failed to meet the needs of the Indian community.

In 1969 a Special Senate Subcommittee on Indian Education chaired by Senator Edward Kennedy concluded that the national policies for the education of Indian children were a "failure of major proportions."[13] Other reports and publications reveal the same grim picture. In ranking tests, Indian children consistently score lower than white children at every grade level. The Indian dropout rate is twice the national average, and the average length of schooling for Indians under federal supervision is slightly more than five years, well behind both blacks and Mexican Americans.

During the sixties, Indians realized that the only way they could overcome these educational deficiencies was to assume the responsibility for educating their own children. The government had failed, to a large extent because of its failure to approach Indian children as Indians. "We have been relegated to a no-man's status," said a young Chippewa activist from northern Michigan. "We are not Indians. We are not whites." Biased textbooks, racism in the operation of schools, and the deliberate attempt to underplay Indian culture, history, and heritage in order to acculturate Indian children into the white man's society had seriously eroded the self-concept of Indian students. "Everywhere," stated another activist at the 1970 Sioux Pow-wow held at Colorado Springs, Colorado, "I see myself portrayed as an ignorant, dirty savage. In school, in books, on television, at the movies—everywhere—until I begin believing I am a savage capable of only one feat: sneaking into wagon trains to massacre white settlers."

In July, 1966, Indians on the Navajo reservation established the Rough Rock Demonstration School, the first Indian-run, Indian-dominated school in the country. Rough Rock employed

[12]"Statistics Concerning Indian Education," U.S. Department of the Interior, fiscal year 1971.

[13]Josephy, Red Power, p. 157, citing a 1969 report of the U.S. Senate Committee on Labor and Public Welfare by the Special Senate Subcommittee on Indian Education.

Navajo teachers and aides, introduced bilingual education, and used course material reflecting the richness of the Navajo culture. It also emphasized parental and community participation in school affairs. So successful was the venture that three years later, the Navajo opened the Navajo Community College. In assuming control of educating its youth, the Navajo recognized two essential points: first, Indians do place a high value on education (for example, it is so highly valued on the Hopi reservation their elementary schools regularly run with a ninety percent attendance rate);[14] and, second, school must be relevant and enhance a student's self-concept.

Since the Rough Rock experiment other tribes have been exploring the path of self-determination in education. They recognize it as a tool to help them preserve their own communities and cultural identities while, at the same time, leading them towards Indian management and control of Indian affairs. In the words of Janet McCloud, a Tulalip and fiery leader of the Washington Fish-In, Indians need "the freedom to educate our children through meaningful education that allows them to grow up to be an Indian adult, instead of trying to make them white shadows."[15]

ECONOMICS

For the American Indian the realities of America's promises have struck deeper and with more poignancy than with perhaps any other minority group. Ideally, the fruits of the free enterprise system are there for all to pick. The realities, however, suggest something else.

Since pacification the American Indian has occupied the lowest rung on the economic ladder. The average annual income of the Indian family today is less than half that of the white family and is substantially less than that of the black family. Unemployment remains a critical problem, varying from twenty to eighty per cent on the 282 Indian reservations under federal jurisdiction. Underemployment, due mainly to the lack of basic job skills, also remains a problem for the approximately

14"The Angry American Indian: Starting Down the Protest Trail," *Time* (February 9, 1970), p. 16.
15"Red Power," *Grand Rapids Press*, January 11, 1970, p. 3A.

300,000 Indians who have left the reservation for the city in recent years. In all, these statistics point to squalid living conditions on the reservations (according to the U.S. Public Health Service about ninety percent of reservation dwellings are substandard) and to Indian ghettos in the poverty sections of the major cities. For the old and young alike (a large proportion are under twenty-five), the realities of stark poverty amidst affluence have sparked a new era of militancy and have led activists to rephrase an old question.

For the American Indian a central reality of life within a white-dominated society is conformity, that insistence on sameness which determines who will or will not share in the affluence of the nation. Those who fit into the White Anglo-Saxon Protestant cultural mold will be assured a decent standard of living; those who deviate from this norm will be denied often the very necessities of life. The question for the Indian, then, has traditionally been whether to assimilate and participate in the Great American Dream or to retain his cultural identity and live in poverty. Within the framework of the recent activism emerging from Indian groups, this question has been changed from one of defeatism to one of pride and self-assertion: How can I adapt to a modern world and still retain my Indian identity? For the Red Power advocates there is an answer.

The answer to this question, however, has not come easily, and it has taken nearly a century to emerge as a viable solution to the so-called "Indian problem." After the Indian wars the tribes were placed on reservations administered by the Department of Interior, which in regarding the Indians as wards of the government tended to be paternalistic, treating the Indians as children incapable of managing their own affairs. The old tribal ways were discouraged, many of them banned, such as Indian religious practices, and the former hunting, fishing, and gathering economies were destroyed. Through treaty obligations the government assumed the responsibility of feeding the Indians and in doing so not only undermined the economic foundation of Indian society, but emasculated the Indian man by depriving him of his traditional role of hunter and provider.

Combined with this spiritual destruction, the government began instituting programs designed to change the Indian by encouraging him to assimilate into white society. Probably the most devastating of these was the Dawes General Allotment Act initiated in 1887. Aimed at ending tribal autonomy and thus at hastening assimilation, the Allotment Act called for the breakup of tribal holdings and the reassignment of private plots to individuals. Accordingly, each Indian adult head of a family was to receive 160 acres and each single adult eighty acres. These lands were to be held in trust for twenty-five years, after which outright ownership was to be granted. Land left over from allotment was to be put up for sale to whites. Many tribes resisted this act, especially in the Southwest, because it cut deeply into Indian land holdings. In 1887 Indians held approximately 138 million acres. By 1934 this number had been cut to 48 million acres.

The Allotment Act failed in its general aim to make the Indian over into a landowner and farmer, a parody of white society. Instead, reservation conditions plummeted. Poverty, squalor, and frustration came to characterize life for the American Indian. In a stopgap measure, and to acknowledge Indian participation in World War I, Congress conferred citizenship on all Indians in 1924 (the Indian Citizen Act). Ten years later, Congress passed the Indian Reorganization Act (the Wheeler-Howard Act of 1934), which brought an end to the allotment policy. In other matters, the Reorganization Act halted further sale of Indian lands and made provisions for recovering them. It also extended financial credit to tribes, encouraged the establishment of constitutional tribal governments, restored freedom of religion, and prompted tribal progress.

Gradually, Indian tribes began responding to the incentives put forth in the Reorganization Act. Tribal governments were formed and reservation conditions began to improve. Following World War II, however, Congressional sympathy for the Indian reversed. Again, as in 1887, Congressional pressure heightened to expedite assimilation and end federal responsibility for the Indians. The Indian Claims Commission to permit Indians to file suit against the government was established in 1946; yet, despite this landmark in Indian affairs, the controversy over federal treaty obligations continued to mount. The storm broke in 1953 when Congress announced its intention to terminate federal relations with the tribes at the earliest possible time.

The Menominees of Wisconsin became the first tribe slated

for termination. Prior to this decision, the Menominees had good schools and community services plus a sawmill owned by the tribe. After termination financial disaster struck the Menominee reservations. Millions of dollars in tribal assets were siphoned into the attempt to create a self-supporting community. County services, including the reservation hospital, became the responsibility of community taxation, and the new and sudden tax burden forced many families to sell their homes. The hospital, faced with a critical loss of funds, shut down. And the operation of the sawmill became unprofitable, forcing tribal managers to automate, a move putting many employees out of work. Almost overnight, the Menominees faced bankruptcy and the state of Wisconsin found itself holding a welfare bill for the tribe six times its previous amount.[16]

While Congress promoted termination, the Bureau of Indian Affairs launched a new program designed to improve the Indian's economic condition by fostering urbanization. The principal aim was to get the Indian off the reservation and into a job in the city, where he could function as a "normal" American citizen. As part of this program of relocation, Indians were interviewed on the reservations, and those individuals and heads of families seeming to possess the ability to adjust to a new life setting were encouraged to emigrate to large metropolitan regions such as Los Angeles and Chicago. They were helped in finding housing and employment—and then left to their own devices. Although many Indians did adjust and move into white society, many others were left stranded, relegated to a poverty status in an alien setting.

The advent of the sixties saw the end of both termination and relocation. From the beginning, the policy of termination had met stiff opposition from the Indians, and the experience of the Menominees, as well as of the Klamaths of Oregon, whose termination had resulted in soaring rates of alcoholism, crime, and suicide, had forced Congress to postpone its hopes for ending federal responsibility to the Indians. Relocation, too, had met bitter opposition, but it was never discontinued officially. Instead, it gradually died off during the Kennedy administration, when new interest was ad-

16 "Angry American Indian, etc.," *Time* (February 9, 1970), p. 18.

vanced towards economic development on the reservation, a theme reaching fruition during the Johnson years.

President Johnson's Great Society program had a dramatic impact on the nation's Indians. For the first time in history they were in a position to design their own programs, apply for funding, and manage these programs as they saw fit. The lesson was a valuable one. As with other minority groups who through the Office of Economic Opportunity's War On Poverty found themselves in a position to determine their own future, Indians proved what they had long been saying, that they could manage their own lives and manage them with more efficiency and efficacy than whites. More importantly, white legislators and bureaucrats discovered that Indians were fully capable of managing reservation matters and handling their own affairs.

Economically, Indians continue to suffer, but this is not necessarily a permanent condition. By uniting and voicing their twin concerns—cultural preservation and economic growth—Indians have been able to move towards an Indian war on poverty. One direction they have started to take is in the development of tribal enterprises, Indian-owned and Indian-operated businesses to bolster reservation economies. Tribes like the Navajo, who have created the Navajo Forest Products Industries, and Washington state's Lummi Indians, who have developed a major aquafarm, recognize the importance of building economic strength from within the reservation. But inner-reservation resources are not always enough. Rejecting such policies as relocation to industrial settings, Indians are working to attract industries to the reservations. In the seven-year period from 1962 to 1969, Indians were able to attract private industry to establish 140 new plants on or near reservations.[17]

The Indians of today have gone a long way toward destroying the stereotype of the beaten nation waiting for the final extinction. They have turned inward to retrieve a sense of pride in their "Indianness" and have determined to retain their background. They have explored the nature of their needs as a nation within a nation and have determined to achieve those needs while remaining a nation within a nation. They have studied the power movements of groups like the blacks and

---

[17]As reported in the October 13, 1969, issue of *Senior Scholastic*, p. 7.

Chicanos, and recognizing the crucial difference that having a land base and treaty obligations makes, have determined to use the power that activism and a united Indian voice create. And they have begun struggling for unity, a unity of old and young alike, to gain the power to control their own destiny.

In answer to the question, How can I adapt to a modern world and still retain my own identity? Red Power advocates are saying, as the United Southeastern Tribes said in a 1969 policy statement, let "the Indian be recognized as the controller of his own destiny both in terms of the direction he chooses and the method of moving in that direction."[18]

[18]Josephy, *Red Power*, p. 146, citing the response of the United Southeastern Tribes (USET) to a proposal that Indian affairs be turned over to state governments.

12

A STUDY OF A RED POWER ORGANIZATION

THEY HAVE BEEN CALLED everything from the "shock troops" of Indian sovereignty to communists. Some Indian leaders consider them the bane of Indian activism. Others claim they are the only true Indians left. But whatever their current status, the members of the American Indian Movement (AIM) remain the most vocal and militant of all Indian reform organizations. Born during the late sixties in southside Minneapolis, AIM has flourished as a seemingly ubiquitous protest movement dedicated to the concept of a "Sovereign Indian America." In that vein, it sees as its major enemies the institutions of traditional Christianity, the American education system, and governmental bureaucracy.

Clyde Bellacourt, a tall Ojibway born on the White Earth Reservation in Minnesota, is generally credited with founding the activist organization. As the story goes, while Clyde was incarcerated in Minnesota's Stillwater State Prison during the early sixties, he suffered a period of extreme depression. The would-be militant had been in trouble most of his life. As a child he had been categorized a juvenile delinquent and had gone through the circuit of state training schools and juvenile reform institutions, where he learned to steal cars. By his late teens he had graduated to burglary. His friends claim that he had been a particularly adept burglar, but he was eventually caught and turned over to state prison authorities. It was several years later, while serving his term at Stillwater, that he realized his life had no direction. "I was convinced," Bellacourt explained, "that I was an ignorant, dirty savage—so I just gave up." He cursed his Indianness, cursed himself, and resolved that he would never eat again. At this point in his life, an Ojibway medicine man named Eddie Benton took an interest in him.

Eddie Benton was descended from a family of Ojibway spiritual leaders. As a trustee at Stillwater, he had access to Bellacourt's cell block. As an Ojibway, and as a spiritual leader himself, he recognized the cause of Bellacourt's despondency. In Benton's words: "The system beats Indian people down. It robs them of their self-respect. It demoralizes and discards them, and too often leads to resignation and defeat." Benton, who had himself experienced this pattern of demoralization, began counselling Bellacourt. He told him about the Ojibway Nation, that the Ojibway people (the white man's corruption being "Chippewa") were once one of the largest Indian groups in North America and had occupied a territory extending from Lake Huron to the Turtle Mountains in North Dakota. He told Bellacourt about the prowess of the Ojibway warriors who had stood against the powerful Iroquoian Nation and had pushed them eastward from the Great Lakes. He extolled the spirituality of the Ojibways, how they had resisted Christianity, and how this spirituality—which regards everything as fitting within a sacred hoop of harmony and unity—had survived 350 years of attack by white society and white missionaries. And finally, he convinced Bellacourt that "To be an Indian in twentieth-century America is to hold the key to survival, for the white man is going headlong towards self-destruction."

A firm friendship grew between the two men. Bellacourt responded by eating again and by reading the numerous books and nationalist literature Benton slipped into his cell. "For the first time in my life," Bellacourt explained, "I realized that I wasn't a savage. I wasn't filthy and I wasn't ignorant. I was smart and capable." Together, Benton and Bellacourt formed an Indian-awareness program aimed at providing Stillwater's Indian inmates with a sense of pride in their Indian heritage. Early in 1964, Bellacourt was paroled and found employment with a power company in Minneapolis. There he settled in the section of southside Minneapolis called the "reservation" because of its large concentration of urban Indians.

The "reservation" covers about twenty square blocks near Minneapolis' Franklin Avenue. It is an urban-renewal area caught in the curious transition between the old and the new. Rundown flats, deteriorating apartment buildings, and shabby Victorian houses exist virtually side by side with the incongruity of modern apartment buildings. About half of the approximately eight to ten thousand Indians in Minneapolis live within this designated region, comprising the largest single geographic concentration of Indians in the Twin Cities area.

Theresa Pindegayosh, a human-resources worker for the Twin Cities Indian Affairs Commission, says, "Most of the people came here on their own or through their relatives being here." A small proportion came through relocation by the Bureau of Indian Affairs.

Relocation succeeded in transplanting hundreds of Indians into the city, but it also opened a Pandora's box of troubles for the new arrivals. As one leader commented, "Indians came into an urban setting ill-equipped to cope with today's society. The society didn't speak his language, didn't understand his cultural background and didn't really care about him as an individual." Ramon Roubideaux, chief legal counsellor for the American Indian Movement, said:

> For the victim of relocation, the sense of alienation in an urban setting was compounded. The BIA had done nothing to prepare him for the complexities of urban life. And when an Indian's first paycheck was also his last, which was not unusual, the victim found himself stranded, the object of yet another white man's promise.

But relocation or not, once in an urban environment, as Roubideaux explained, Indians usually "seek out other Indian people, settling within an urban Indian ghetto." Faced with an alien culture, often depressed, experiencing discrimination and prejudice, many Indians have difficulty coping and turn to alcohol as a way out. Although accurate figures are difficult to find, Indian leaders say that alcoholism has been one of the most persistent problems their people face.

There are other problems, of course. According to the Upper Midwest American Indian Center, located in Minneapolis, in 1973 about sixty-five percent of the Indian labor force in the "reservation" (the Powderhorn Area for census purposes) was unemployed. Three out of four of those employed fit into the *unskilled* labor category. Housing patterns were unstable, with a mobility rate exceeding fifty percent, and educational under-achievement and high school dropout rates remained critical problems. "An Indian with a degree is at a premium," said Ignatia Broker of the Upper Midwest Center. Underlying these figures and statistics are the human realities of poverty—hunger, disease, high infant-mortality rates, frustration, a pervading sense of failure, and the inevitable breakdown in police-community relations.

In 1964, when Clyde Bellacourt returned to Minneapolis (as a youth he had drifted to Minneapolis after leaving Minnesota's White Earth Reservation), he discovered that the urban condition of the Twin Cities' Indian population had deteriorated greatly from what he could remember of his days before Still-water State Prison. As he settled in the ghetto near Franklin Avenue and assumed the daily routine of working for the power company, his thoughts turned increasingly to the Indian community around him. He learned that there were nearly thirty Indian organizations in the Twin Cities area, and that most of these organizations were having little impact in alleviating the problems of the urban Indians. He also learned that there were other Indians in Minneapolis equally concerned, especially about the seemingly growing harassment of Indian people by area police.

Eddie Benton, the spiritual leader who had helped Bella-court at Stillwater and later became director of the American Indian Movement in St. Paul, said, "The one particular thing that finally kicked AIM into being, into birth, was police brutality against Indian people. The whole Indian community of south Minneapolis just got sick and tired of being beat up and getting their ribs kicked in and their heads busted." Early in 1968, Bellacourt and another ex-con, Dennis Banks, called a meeting with area Indians. They formed what was called a Concerned Indian Citizens Coalition to deal with police brutal-ity and to work on the problems facing the urban Indian community. The coalition was to be a "grass roots" organization run by and for Minneapolis Indians.

By summer the coalition had changed its name to the Concerned Indian Americans (CIA). In July it became a structured organization, a nonprofit corporation with an Indian board and staff. Through the suggestion of several women members, the name was changed to the American Indian Movement, and Clyde Bellacourt was elected the first national director.

One of the first actions AIM took was to create the AIM Patrol, an all-Indian "watchdog" force to guard against police brutality. Members monitored police calls. When a call involving Indians came over the police scanner, the Patrol—its members wearing red jackets with black thunderbird emblems on the back—rushed to the scene to witness and photograph the arrest. In this way AIM documented actual cases of brutality and instituted several law suits against the Minneapolis Police Department. Ultimately, police-community relations improved.

AIM turned to other problems affecting the Indian community in Minneapolis. It instituted an alcohol rehabilitation program and encouraged other Minneapolis Indian organizations to do the same. It opened an all-Indian school, the Red Schoolhouse, designed to help students having difficulties in the public school system. Eddie Benton explained, "Our school runs from pre-school to senior high and works with drop-outs, force-outs, and kick-outs who can't make it in the public school system or are victims of the juvenile court system." AIM formed an Indian health board and later began offering emergency housing and welfare services. It organized an Indian youth program, opened a day-care center, and inaugurated a feeding program. But the real purpose of AIM transcended the Indian ghetto of southside Minneapolis. From its inception, AIM leaders planned for the organization to be an instrument of social change.

"I think that all of the injustices that have been occurring to Indian people led me to believe that Indian people would have to take a stand or perish," said Dennis Banks. "I elected not to perish and elected to make a stand. In Minneapolis, we organized the American Indian Movement to take such a stand." Eddie Benton explained:

We're in the business of political confrontation with the

goal being social change and the philosophy being Indian self-determination. Within the framework of the system of this country, whether that be social or political, the system has not worked for the Indian people. In fact, it has worked against Indian people. It has deprived them of their civil rights, of their land, equality, and it has deprived them of their human rights. The system is stacked against an Indian living the life style of his choosing and pursuing the goals he wishes to pursue.

AIM leaders will say that the purpose of the organization is Indian self-determination. They also explain that AIM is a spiritual movement. As one leader said, "To be an Indian is to be spiritual." Within this context, early in the movement's history the leadership realized that something was lacking. "To the Indian, identification with a protest group is alien," said Ramon Roubideaux. "There has to be a greater identification such as the identification with Indian people, or *Indianness*, and the essence of *Indianness* is spirituality."

AIM leaders heard of a young medicine man in South Dakota named Leonard Crowdog, and they went to visit him. In their first meeting on the Sioux Rosebud Reservation, Leonard Crowdog (grandson of the Crow Dog who had assassinated the famed Brule chief Spotted Tail in 1881) told them that many Indian people had lost their identity. He said that Indian people had become rootless, soul-less persons caught in the cultural limbo between white and Indian society, and he urged the AIM leadership to redefine themselves in Indian terms.

"After we found Leonard," explained an AIM member who refused permission to use his name in fear of FBI reprisal, "other spiritual leaders came forward. We'd thought the old religion had died, but in the hills and on the reservations certain people had kept the traditions alive, locked inside their memories, just waiting for the day when they could give them back to the Indian people." When asked what the old religion was, he explained:

> We live within a sacred cycle, the sacred hoop. We are born from Mother Earth and we return to Mother Earth. We feed on the deer who, in turn, feeds on the grass which, in turn, is fed by our bodies after we die. It's the story of the

biological cycle you learned in school. Everything is harmony and unity, and we fit within that harmony. And when our bodies die, our spirits are freed and will be here. You see, it's not a religion in the white man's sense, but a philosophy of living, a way of living.

Christianity as a philosophy, AIM leaders say, is not inconsistent with Indian philosophy. It teaches love and brotherhood. The church, however, is seen as a villain. "The missionaries came to our country," said Dennis Banks, "and they stole our religion and our land. They stole our children and shaved their heads and sent them to boarding schools. They tried to steal our culture and make us white men." Eddie Benton explained:

We want to make the churches realize what they have done to Indian people. They have worked at times hand-in-hand and in conspiracy with big government and big business to deprive Indian people of their land, their mineral rights, their water rights. The churches are some of the biggest land owners in Indian country.

A second villain seen by the American Indian Movement is the Bureau of Indian Affairs. Dennis Banks: "I spent two and a half years in prison and it was while I was in prison that I realized that the greatest criminal of all was the Bureau of Indian Affairs—and it was allowed to go free." Ramon Roubideaux, who grew up on the Rosebud Sioux Reservation, said, "I realized after twenty years that there weren't going to be any meaningful changes in Indian affairs because we were under the monopolistic, suffocating grip of the Bureau of Indian Affairs."

In 1784 Congress placed the administration of Indian affairs within the War Department. Forty years later, federal Indian activities were lumped together under an Indian Affairs Agency which saw its role as: (1) appropriating tribal annuities; (2) examining Indian claims; (3) bookkeeping and maintaining ties with Indian superintendents and agents; and (4) administering a fund for the "civilization" of Indians. The Indian Affairs Agency remained within the War Department until 1849, when the Department of the Interior was created. That same year the Bureau of Indian Affairs passed from military to civil control, when Congress transferred it to the Department of the Interior.

"From its inception," said AIM leader Russell Means, "the BIA proved to be a mismanaged and bureaucratic federal agency." To this, Dennis Banks added, "The BIA was formed in 1849 to act as trustee for Indian lands. At that time, Indian people held over 150 million acres of land. Now, Indian land has dwindled to 50 million acres. That's how the BIA acted as trustee."

The corruption and incompetency of Indian agents in the past are among the many shortcomings AIM sees in the BIA. AIM also sees the BIA as a bureaucratic agency struggling for its life against other bureaucratic agencies, a condition which AIM leaders say makes the BIA more responsive to white Congressmen than to Indian people. Another bone of contention with AIM is the fact that none of the 371 treaties between the Indian tribes and the United States government made provision for the BIA administration of Indian affairs. "The treaties never spelled out that there would be a Bureau of Indian Affairs to dictate to us," explained Ramon Roubideaux, "and as long as the BIA remains, we can only look forward to being enslaved."

Thus, AIM has committed itself to war. "The American Indian Movement after Wounded Knee," said Russell Means, "began to adopt a better policy aimed at abolishing the BIA." Dennis Banks explained this further: "The Bureau of Indian Affairs dictates to us from the moment we are born to the moment we die, and AIM will not rest until that government agency is totally and completely destroyed."

As the institutions of organized Christianity and governmental bureaucracy are seen as enemies by AIM, so is the institution of the American education system. "The schools have been our biggest enemies," said Ramon Roubideaux. "From racism to a cultural rip-off to the implantation of racial inferiority, the educational process has tried to make us into a nation of children—and white children, at that." Another AIM member, an Ojibway from Michigan, said, "We have a seventy-five percent dropout rate in schools, and it's not because Indians are stupid."

Because AIM leaders feel that irrelevancy in the traditional educational system is at fault, AIM has promoted its own schools. They are called "survival schools" and concentrate on what is termed *survival skills* meant to enable a student to survive in both Indian communities and white society. They employ Indian teachers and, in addition to the formalized studies of reading, writing, and arithmetic, they stress the study of Indian history and Indian culture. "They are bilingual, bicultural schools," said Eddie Benton, "taught in the Indian way." These schools are an outgrowth of the Red Schoolhouse concept originated in the Twin Cities, and AIM leaders say they have proven successful.

Yet, AIM as an organization is noted today more for its militancy than for its educational programs. Controversy, criticism, and confrontation are the qualities usually associated with the American Indian Movement, and AIM has lived up to this reputation. In 1972 the image of AIM changed dramatically. This came, says Ramon Roubideaux, "when we pushed into the area of civil rights for all Indian people and not just for urban Indians."

And by 1972 AIM had received national recognition. Dennis Banks gives much of the credit for the organization's rise to prominence to Clyde Bellacourt: "It was because of Clyde's aggressiveness that he was elected as first chairman of AIM, and it was through his organizing efforts that the American Indian Movement became a national organization." In that same year, AIM accelerated the tempo of confrontation against the white establishment, and a series of incidents climaxed in November's week-long occupation of the Bureau of Indian Affairs building in Washington, D.C.

"We really got it on in Washington," said Dennis Banks— and, indeed, the organization did. In early November approximately 500 Indian men, women, and children descended on Washington in what was called the Trail of Broken Treaties. Within days of their arrival, they had taken over the BIA building, proclaiming it the "Native American Embassy." In the week-long occupation of that building, militants brandished war clubs and pistols. They painted their faces and moved to the sound of war drums. Inside the building, demonstrators smashed furniture and typewriters and carted off part of an Indian art collection and cartons full of government documents. At occupation's end, damage to the building and contents exceeded $2 million.

Prior to the November march, AIM had been in Flagstaff, Arizona, to protest the Flagstaff Chamber of Commerce's exploitation of Indians during the annual POWWOW Days held there. AIM had also been in Gordon, Nebraska, trying to force an investigation into the killing of a fifty-one-year-old Sioux, Raymond Yellow Thunder. And the organization had taken over a Naval Air Guard station in Minneapolis to press claims for federal land. But the march on Washington was by far its most controversial action. The reasons for the demonstration were many, but they centered around three main points.

1. AIM supporters needed to bring public attention to the deplorable conditions affecting the approximately 800,000 Native Americans in the United States.
2. AIM leaders needed a show of solidarity among Indian people to dramatize the growing impatience of the Red Man in America.
3. AIM needed a public platform from which it could orate its principal demand—that Indian people be dealt with as a sovereign nation that has never relinquished its sovereignty.

The result of AIM's militancy in the Capital was mixed. The organization succeeded in swinging public attention to the Indian for awhile, but it also unleashed a barrage of criticism not only from Congress but from other Indians as well. Although many Indians supported AIM, many of the more conservative Indian leaders quite vocally disavowed the organization and called its members "Maoists" and "revolutionaries." As for AIM's demands, the federal government agreed to set up a study group to look into the matter and then paid transportation for the demonstrators to return to their homes.

Back home for many of the demonstrators was Minneapolis. For others it was any of a number of cities with large Indian populations. Still others returned to reservations. In the four-year history of AIM, it had spread to include nearly forty chapters on various reservations and in urban areas, including Denver and Los Angeles.

But once at home, AIM was not content to sit on its success in Washington. Within three months a few of AIM's leaders had journeyed to Custer, South Dakota, to protest, in Ramon Roubideaux's words, "a double standard of justice in South Dakota."

In the weeks preceding AIM's arrival, a white man had knifed an Indian, Wesley Bad Heart, in the Buffalo Gap Bar near Custer. The incident followed a disagreement between the two men several days earlier, a disagreement in which the assailant had threatened to kill Wesley Bad Heart. The threat had been witnessed, yet, after the killing, the assailant had been charged with second-degree manslaughter.

The AIM leadership was furious. "After all," said Ramon Roubideaux, "an Indian in the same circumstances would have been charged with murder." So AIM went to Custer on February 6, 1973, and in the zero-degree weather of a South Dakota winter mustered a protest demonstration. AIM tried to get the prosecutor to change the charge. When that failed the demonstrators set fire to the courthouse. The courthouse blaze was immediately extinguished by the Custer Fire Department. Meanwhile, other demonstrators managed to burn down the Chamber of Commerce building.

Custer's prosecuting attorney finally agreed to an investigation into the killing. Ramon Roubideaux was put in charge of the investigation and enlisted the aid of Fred Gabourie, an Indian attorney from Los Angeles. "Before we could complete our investigation and make our report," maintains Roubideaux, "they hurriedly called the case to trial and tried it with a Custer County jury. They acquitted the guy and we never did have a say on what the charge should be."

Meanwhile, on the Pine Ridge Indian Reservation near Custer, members of the Oglala Sioux tribe requested assistance from AIM in ousting their tribal council president, Richard Wilson. The charges against Wilson included misuse of tribal funds, receiving kickbacks from a Rapid City construction firm, raising his own salary against the wishes of the tribal council, and employing members of his family in choice council jobs. According to AIM, the Oglalas had tried to impeach Wilson four times in the preceding year, the last attempt coming early in February, 1973, at which time Wilson presided over his own impeachment and ruled himself innocent of all charges.

After the failure of the last impeachment attempt, AIM

says, the Oglalas called upon their three traditional chiefs to take action. These chiefs then called upon the American Indian Movement for help, and AIM met with the Oglalas on February 25, 26, and 27. "It was at the February 27 meeting," said Dennis Banks, "that we were approached by two Oglala women—Gladys Bissionette and Ellen Moves Camp—who cried and begged the traditional chiefs to make a move." Banks said that the two women "demanded to know where the Indian men were, demanded to know if there were any Indian men left." As the February 27 meeting continued, Banks explained, the small meeting hall at Calico became filled, "and we decided to move to another community hall at Porcupine."

Midway between the communities of Calico and Porcupine sits the small village of Wounded Knee, site of the 1890 massacre of 200 Indian men, women, and children by the 7th U.S. Cavalry. Enroute to Porcupine, the Oglalas and AIM leaders stopped at Wounded Knee to visit the mass gravesite there. "While we were at the gravesite," said Banks, "we recognized that we could go no further. We had to stay there at Wounded Knee and make our stand. And we decided we would never leave Wounded Knee until some kind of justice came to Indian country."

The armed occupation of Wounded Knee, South Dakota, officially began on Tuesday, February 27. By Wednesday the area had been surrounded by U.S. marshalls and FBI agents and a grim stalemate settled over the four square miles which AIM declared had seceded from the United States. Vernon Bellacourt, co-director with his brother Clyde of the American Indian Movement and a national field director, stayed away from the occupied region in order to publicize AIM's demands. In essence, they were these:

1. the removal of Richard Wilson as president of the Oglala Sioux tribal council;
2. a Congressional investigation of the Bureau of Indian Affairs;
3. recognition of the 1868 Fort Laramie Treaty;
4. an investigation into the matter of the 371 broken treaties; and
5. recognition of the sovereignty of Indian people.

The occupation lasted over two months and netted little more than publicity and criminal indictments against more than a hundred members of the American Indian Movement. Both sides laid down their weapons on May 8, after the chiefs and headmen of the Oglala Sioux signed an agreement with the federal government. In return for an end to the siege, the government promised: (1) to investigate the charges against Wilson; and (2) to hold treaty meetings with the Oglalas in order to review the 1868 Fort Laramie Treaty.

After Wounded Knee, the participants in the siege disbanded and returned to their homes around the country. Said one AIM member, a law student from Los Angeles, "I feel we accomplished something. At least I accomplished something—I was ready to die for a cause."

Many of those leaving the Pine Ridge reservation did so knowing they would have to return to South Dakota to stand trial in Sioux Falls on nonconspiracy charges ranging from breaking and entering to grand larceny. For the two leaders of the siege, Dennis Banks and Russell Means, the standdown on May 8 was merely a prelude to the weeks and months ahead. Both Banks and Means faced charges of conspiracy. The trial, which AIM called the "trial of the century," began January 8, 1974, in St. Paul, Minnesota, and dragged on for more than eight months before all charges against Means and Banks were dismissed on the grounds of government misconduct.

The American Indian Movement remains the foremost Indian activist organization. Born from the frustration of life in an urban Indian ghetto, AIM rose to national stature within the relatively short span of four years. AIM leaders contend that their activism in the past is a pattern for the future. They maintain that they will not rest until justice does come to Indian country, and justice includes overcoming the so-called traditional enemies of Indian people—organized Christianity, the Bureau of Indian Affairs, and the mis-education of Indian children. As Martin Luther King, Jr., had a dream, so does the American Indian Movement. In Vernon Bellacourt's words: "We will not rest until every Indian nation is sovereign and represented in an Indian United Nations." In order to accomplish this, Dennis Banks says, "Indian people can no longer remain weekend warriors. The war goes on in the courts. The war goes on in the school systems. The war goes on in the BIA in Washington. The longest war continues."

13

INDIAN LEADERS

VINE DELORIA, JR.

THERE IS NO SINGLE INDIAN LEADER who speaks for all Native Americans. There are too many tribal bodies, languages, and customs for that. Rather, there are tribal leaders and organizational leaders who sometimes manage to voice the concerns of most Native Americans, but who more often speak for segments of the Indian population or for special-interest groups. If there is any Indian spokesman, however, who approaches a degree of universality extending across tribal barriers and differences, it would probably be Vine Deloria, Jr. The former executive director of the National Congress of American Indians and author of two explosive manifestos, *Custer Died for Your Sins* and *We Talk, You Listen,* Deloria has eloquently, and with biting humor, put into words the concerns, frustrations, and goals of the American Indian.

Vine Deloria, Jr., was born in 1933 in Martin, South Dakota, a town which borders the Pine Ridge Indian reservation. His father was an Episcopalian missionary, as was his grandfather, and young Vine's earliest experiences were a mixture of Christianity and Indian traditionalism. When he was seventeen, his family moved to Iowa; shortly thereafter, the young spokesman joined the Marines. After his hitch in the service, Deloria went to the seminary, but he was never ordained because, as he explains, he lost faith in the "white man's religion." Instead, he went to work for the United Scholarship Service, an organization promoting the college and secondary school education of Indian and Chicano students. At the age of thirty, Deloria was elected executive director of the National Congress of American Indians.

As director of the NCAI, Deloria at first approached the problems besetting Native Americans in the pattern established by his predecessors. He attended conferences, worked with government agencies, and helped formulate numerous policies, proposals, and plans designed to magically solve the so-called "Indian problem." By 1967, however, he saw that "running the conference circuit," as he calls it, had not proven effective. Indian leaders who had been working at the local levels, either on reservations or in urban Indian ghettos, were garnering far greater successes in improving the Indian economic and social condition. These leaders, Deloria realized, had been able to consolidate whole communities into single units, which were then able to use this unity as an effective weapon to influence local white politicians. And with this unity came a sense of sharing, and a sense of pride in "Indianness."

Indian self-determination—that was what the new Indian leaders were saying; and Deloria recognized the power behind that phrase. Late in 1967 he entered law school because, as he explains, the new Indian revolution would desperately need legal representation. Meanwhile, he wrote *Custer Died for Your Sins: An Indian Manifesto,* which proved an overwhelming success. Overnight, Deloria received national and international acclaim as the Standing Rock Sioux with the biting wit. On the heels of this first success came *We Talk, You Listen,* in which he levied a head-on attack against the problems of American society. Somehow, along with his first two books, his rigorous schedule calling for speeches, magazine articles, and interviews, and attendance at numerous Indian conferences, he also managed to earn a law degree from the University of Colorado.

Recognized as one of the foremost spokesmen for Indian people, Deloria has also been accepted as a spokesman for all oppressed minority people. He has been a member of the Board of Inquiry on Hunger and Malnutrition in the U.S.A. and of the National Office for the Rights of the Indigent. As such, he has earned a reputation as a leader able to voice the concerns of Mexican Americans, blacks, poor whites, and even religious

minorities like the Amish. But, if he is to be remembered by history, it will probably be as an Indian leader. Indian people remain fractionalized, divided, but they are moving towards unity—at least on some fronts. Vine Deloria, Jr., is one of the leaders calling for this unity.

VERNON BELLACOURT

He is an ex-con, an ex-beautician, an ex-real estate salesman; if he had his way, he'd be an ex-United States citizen. He is Vernon Bellacourt, a national field director for the American Indian Movement.

Vernon Bellacourt was born on October 17, 1931, on the White Earth Reservation in Minnesota. One of twelve children in his family, he dropped out of school in the ninth grade. At the age of fifteen, he left the reservation and drifted to Minneapolis. By the time he was twenty he had turned to crime, because, as he explains, he was bitter against society's systematic destruction of Indian people. Motivated by confusion, hostility, and revenge, he became a fairly adept thief. He was finally caught and sent to prison for armed robbery. He was paroled, only to be arrested for another crime. He served three and a half years, was paroled a second time, and returned to Minneapolis to open a beauty salon. By this time he was in his mid-twenties.

For more than fifteen years, Bellacourt submerged himself in white society. As Mr. Vernon of Minneapolis, he was a well-known hair stylist. He then went into the import business, and for a while was in real estate. But beneath the exterior of a successful businessman "making it" in white suburbia, Bellacourt felt empty, gnawed by a sense that he was moving in the wrong direction. In 1969 he took a week's vacation and visited his brother Clyde, one of the founders of the American Indian Movement.

When Bellacourt visited his brother, who was then the national director of the fledgling movement, he began to re-identify with his Indian heritage. He let his hair grow long, discarded his "white" business suit, tried to erase his fifteen years as an "assimilated" Indian, and, he stoically comments, separated from his "white" wife. By 1972 he had been elected

National Codirector of AIM and had established a headquarters in Denver. That November he went to Washington, D.C., to participate in the Trail of Broken Treaties. When the siege at Wounded Knee broke out the following spring, he remained away in order to act as spokesman and rally support for his besieged brothers.

Because he is a spokesman, Vernon Bellacourt has become a symbol of Indian militancy. He is tall, wears his hair in braids, and speaks with an intense dignity. Born of Ojibway blood, he nevertheless speaks of Indian unity. One of his main goals is to have Indian people declared sovereign and thus be seated as an independent nation in the United Nations.

MEL THOM

They've called him "Little Bear." They've called him "Smokey the Bear." A few of his more ardent fans—and enemies— have called him "Mao Tse Thom." He is a short, stocky Paiute and a graduate civil engineer. He was for several years the fiery voice of Indian youth, of that determined and active segment of American Indians who, somewhat with tongue in cheek, called themselves the Red Muslims.

Mel Thom was born on July 28, 1938, on the Walker River Reservation in Nevada. As a Paiute he grew up in a cultural atmosphere stressing the strong and proud traditions of the Walker River band. His people were one of the last tribes to give up the fight against the U.S. government. (Their final battle was fought in the year 1911 on the alkali flats of the Nevada desert.) Their heroes are many, including Wovoka, the prophet who inspired the famous Sioux Ghost Dances. These traditions and the tribalism of the Walker River Paiutes etched themselves deeply into his character and underlie his personal philosophy for Indian people.

As a boy, Thom explains with a deep chuckle, he worked as a cowpuncher. Later, he moved into construction, and by the time he reached his latter teens, he had decided to become a civil engineer. At the age of nineteen, he enrolled in Brigham Young University at Provo, Utah. Four years later, during the summer of 1961, he traveled to Chicago to attend an American Indian Conference at the University of Chicago.

There were several young Indian leaders at the Chicago conference, and they soon grew disenchanted with the rhetoric

of what they termed the "Uncle Tomahawks." They formed a youth caucus and prepared a Statement of Purpose, declaring that Indian people have the right of self-government and sovereignty. Ten of these young leaders met that August at the Inter-tribal Ceremonial held at Gallup, New Mexico.

The purpose of the Gallup meeting was to form a new movement which would involve Indian youth in the preservation of Indian values and in the move towards self-determination. The movement was named the National Indian Youth Council, and Mel Thom was elected council president. "The Indian people are going to remain Indians for a long time to come," Thom wrote that day in the movement's Statement of Purpose; he added: "Being of Indian origin should always be held in high regard but never as a disadvantage."[19]

The same year, Thom graduated from Brigham Young as a civil engineer and returned to his reservation, where he was elected tribal chairman. Meanwhile, he continued voicing the concept of the new tribalism which rejected assimilation in favor of retaining a strong Indian identity. "We do not want to be pushed into the mainstream life," Thom said in a speech delivered at the American Indian Capital Conference on Poverty in May of 1964. "We want to remain Indian people." He went on to maintain, "We are not going to disappear . . . we are here to stay. . . ."[20]

In the seven years that he was chairman of the National Indian Youth Council, Thom crisscrossed the country from Washington, D.C., to Washington State delivering his message of Indian self-determination and Indian awareness. He testified on subcommittees on poverty, helped organize protest movements like the Washington Fish-In, and spoke at universities and Indian conferences. His voice was one of the strongest advocating the Red Power Movement. Then in 1968, he resigned from the NIYC and decided to devote his time primarily to the people of his own reservation.

Since then, Mel Thom has lived as a reservation Indian, becoming chairman of the Walker River Reservation. "I have enough to do right here," he said in an October, 1973, interview, "taking care of things at home."

19Steiner, *New Indians*, p. 305.
20Josephy, *Red Power*, p. 55.

14

INDIAN ORGANIZATIONS

THERE ARE AS MANY Indian organizations as there are Indian groups. Most deal with local issues on a regional scale. Nearly every urban center where there is a countable Indian population has its intertribal council, Indian affairs commission, or Indian center. Reservation Indians also have their organizations, which may confine themselves to a single reservation or reach out to include a larger area, perhaps several reservations. A few organizations have grown to national stature, and these organizations have largely been able to cut across tribal boundaries and speak, at least on occasion, for a broad spectrum of Native Americans. Each of these national organizations is trying to unify Indian people and break down the traditional fragmentation between tribes and groups which has hampered Indian reform movements in the past. In addition, each of these organizations is committed to the concept of Indian self-determination.

Gerald Wilkinson, executive director of the National Indian Youth Council, comments, "There's a lot of ways up the mountain and every organization has to do its part while finding its own way up." The top of the mountain, of course, is an Indian America where Native Americans can retain their Indianness and yet benefit from twentieth-century technology. The path to the top, the tactics used, can vary as much as Indian people can vary.

THE AMERICAN INDIAN HISTORICAL SOCIETY

The American Indian Historical Society (AIHS) was formed in 1964 by a group of Indian intellectuals to counter the stereotypes of ignorance and savagery which have plagued Native Americans since Jamestown. Initially, AIHS printed a small mimeographed newsletter extolling Indian history. Soon the organization began exerting pressure on publishers to correct the Indian image in textbooks, and to present an authentic account of Indian history. By 1970, AIHS had founded an Indian press and had sponsored the first meeting of Indian scholars.

Today the American Indian Historical Society publishes its own historical material while maintaining pressure on other publishing firms to print the truth. The newsletter, which had originally been intended to challenge the white academic community to take a closer look at Indian history, has grown into a quarterly having a broader impact. In addition, AIHS continues to promote Indian scholarship.

THE AMERICAN INDIAN MOVEMENT

The American Indian Movement (AIM) was formed in 1968 in Minneapolis, Minnesota, in response to police harassment and poverty-related problems which affect urban Indians. AIM became a national organization within four years and quickly proved itself the most activist of current Indian organizations. In November, 1972, AIM helped sponsor the Trail of Broken Treaties, the Indian march on Washington, D.C., which led to the week-long occupation of the Bureau of Indian Affairs building. In February, 1973, AIM participated in the siege at Wounded Knee, South Dakota. The occupation of the small village on the Pine Ridge Indian Reservation lasted more than two months and pitted armed Indian militants against U.S. marshalls and FBI agents. The siege ended on May 8, after the federal government agreed to investigate charges of corruption against Richard Wilson, president of the Oglala Sioux tribal council. The government also agreed to hold treaty meetings with the Oglala headmen to review the 1868 treaty with their nation.

The American Indian Movement has been the subject of much criticism from both Indian and white leaders. Yet, AIM leaders say they will continue in their hard line against injustice and promise more demonstrations in the future. AIM's goal is to create what it calls a Sovereign Indian America.

AMERICANS FOR INDIAN OPPORTUNITY

Americans for Indian Opportunity (AIO) is a national non-profit organization designed to promote Indian self-help programs and to educate the general public about Native Americans. The AIO is made up of both Indians and non-Indians. Its president is Mrs. Fred R. (LaDonna) Harris, a Comanche from Oklahoma and the wife of former Senator Harris. The organization's headquarters is in Washington, D.C.

The AIO sees as one of its principal goals helping Indians at the local level. As such, it prefers to initiate local programs and turn them over to local organizations. Included in these local programs are agencies established to provide small business loans and technical assistance to Indian entrepreneurs, agencies active in educational counseling for Indian youth, and agencies willing to run Indian centers for rural and urban Indian populations. The AIO maintains a legal defense fund for the twin purposes of educating Native Americans about their legal rights and for acting as a watchdog against discrimination. As with other Indian organizations, the AIO is committed to Indian self-determination and gears its assistance to that end.

THE NATIONAL CONGRESS OF AMERICAN INDIANS

The years of World War II were precarious years for American Indian policy. Indians had no national organization to speak for them, and with public and Congressional attention focused on international conditions, the field of Indian affairs had been swept aside by policy-makers. A number of Indian intellectuals realized that this situation could very well establish the pattern for future relations with Congress. Under the urging of the Commissioner of Indian Affairs, John Collier, a meeting was held in November, 1944. Tribal and religious leaders from across the United States and Indian leaders from the Bureau of Indian Affairs attended the two-day conference held in Denver,

Colorado. At that meeting the National Congress of American Indians (NCAI) was born.

In the first policy-making meeting, the representatives wanted the NCAI to confine itself to broad problems affecting either all Indians or large groups of Indian people. The initial leadership felt that meeting problems on the local level—unless such problems had large-scale implications—would weaken the organization by diffusing its power. It was also decided that the NCAI should deal in the areas of legislation and the protection of legal rights.

In its early years, the NCAI exerted pressure on Congress to establish the Indian Claims Commission. It fought hard to get the Navajo-Hopi Rehabilitation Act passed. But its greatest test came a decade after its founding, when Congress instituted the hated termination policy.

The NCAI reacted quickly to this threat and called an emergency meeting of its members. For two months, Indian leaders from dozens of tribes remained in the Capital to protest termination. When they returned to their homes, the NCAI continued to lobby against the policy. Finally, termination was abandoned, the NCAI being instrumental in this decision.

The NCAI's stand against termination enhanced its stature among Indians, and tribal membership in the organization grew. Today the National Congress of American Indians remains the most important Indian civil rights organization. Despite problems in funding and internal factionalism, the NCAI continues to be a strong force in the area of Indian legislation. It is committed to Indian self-determination and sees itself as a force meant to protect Indian lands and resources.

THE NATIONAL INDIAN YOUTH COUNCIL

In June, 1961, the National Congress of American Indians and the University of Chicago sponsored the American Indian Chicago Conference to bring Indian leaders together in order to formulate a united policy proposal for presentation to the Kennedy administration. At the convention a number of youthful members of the NCAI met and formed a youth caucus to represent the voice of Indian youth at the meetings. After the convention ended, several of these young leaders agreed to meet in August at Gallup, New Mexico. On August 10, ten members of the Chicago youth caucus met in Gallup's Indian Community Center and formed the National Indian Youth Council (NIYC).

From its inception the NIYC adopted a more liberal and aggressive stance than its parent organization, the NCAI. One of its first mass actions was participation in the Washington State Fish-Ins in 1964. The same year, the NIYC took over sponsorship of the United Scholarship Service, an organization designed to give assistance and scholarship aid to Indians and Mexican American youth.

Although originally created as a vehicle for the voice of Indian youth, the NIYC now includes members of all ages. Much of the work done by the organization is in education. The NIYC established the first Indian-controlled school in Oklahoma. It operates summer workshops at major universities (the Clyde Warrior Institute in American Indian Studies), and maintains an intern program for Indian students to work in federal offices in Washington, D.C. One of its major concerns is student rights. At present the NIYC encourages the use of a Student Bill of Rights applicable to Indian boarding schools.

Besides education, the organization is involved in civil rights activities. It has fought land development on reservations, has sued the Oklahoma Supreme Court for jury selection procedures, and has brought discrimination suits against a number of agencies, including the Bureau of Indian Affairs.

In the area of action research, the NIYC is concerned with the manipulations of private business interests as they apply to federal and state reservations. Currently, the NIYC is investigating the influences of agri-business and organized crime on Indian reservations.

15
INDIANS OF THE UNITED STATES

THE WISCONSIN ERA OF GLACIATION began about 75,000 years ago, and the ice sheets advanced to cover nearly all of Canada and portions of the United States. During this time enough sea water was locked into the ice to lower the ocean level by several hundred feet. Because the lowering of the sea level by twenty fathoms would expose a land bridge between Siberia and Alaska across the Bering Strait, it is probable that a dry-land passageway existed throughout most of this era, perhaps even as recently as 10,000 years ago.

What followed, according to most experts, is that small nomadic bands of humans following the migratory patterns of big-game animals wandered across this connecting stretch of land (often called *Beringia*), into a New World. They did so out of hunger, obeying hunting patterns established by thousands of generations of forebears.

As a big-game hunter, man filtered southward along corridors between the glaciers, and once below the massive ice sheets spread over the virgin land of his new home. This migration—which can only be viewed as a migration within the context of thousands of years—was probably slow and random.

At first his stone and bone implements were large and crudely made, but as new generations poured forth over the new land, his weapons and tools gained precision and form. He learned to chip and flatten spear points, creating sharp weapons capable of penetrating the tough hides of animals many times his size. He built traps and used fire to drive his prey into these traps. He learned to chip stone knives and scrapers, enabling him to butcher his kill quicker, and to cure the hide for clothing and shelter.

On the fringe of this big-game technology, a few tribes took to food-gathering as a primary means of survival. Most tribes, however, remained as their ancestors had—a nomadic culture based on a hunting economy. They hunted small game, and gathered roots, berries, and other herbs only to augment their regular diets. Then, with a finality that puzzles scientists even today, the giant prehistoric mammals disappeared.

Whatever caused their demise, the extinction of the mammoth, the ground sloth, the camel, the horse, and other creatures in the New World had a profound impact upon the life-style of these ancient Indians. They now had to rely on small game and natural foods for survival. This led to new ways of hunting and new weapons like the snare and the bow and arrow. To gather wild foods they needed carrying implements, and bowls and baskets were invented. Perhaps the most significant development was agriculture. Indians began planting crops, and slowly the nomadic way of life gave way to a more settled, regionalized existence. Beliefs and philosophies also underwent revisions, and gradually the Indians developed new cultures and new societies.

INDIANS OF THE NORTHEAST WOODLANDS

As the great ice sheets receded from what is now the northeastern United States, the climate warmed. Patches of vegetation followed this retreat, and gradually the Northeast became forestland capable of supporting human life.

The regionalization of the Northeast probably began around 5,000 years ago. Along the western Great Lakes, Indians learned to hammer and shape raw copper to use as ornaments, weapons, and tools. East of this Old Copper Culture was the Lamoka Culture of New York, which used bone and antler for knives, scrapers, and other tools. New York also held the Laurentian Culture, which used harpoons and slate knives and points. Although these early cultures—and there were several others—lived in much the same way as had their ancestors, there were some significant changes, the most marked involving burial customs.

Archaeologists have unearthed evidence showing that around 4,000 years ago these early Indians began to observe increased ceremony in the ritual of burial. Cremation increased and burial offerings became more elaborate. Also during this time the practice of burying the dead in flexed positions in pits and mounds evolved.

The practice of burying the dead in mounds led to the rise of mound-building cultures. The most important of these cultures during this early period was the Adena, which flourished in the Ohio Valley from about 1000 B.C. to approximately A.D. 200. During this same period, agriculture reached the Northeast from Mexico.

As nothing had before, agriculture made a dramatic impact on the life-style of these early Indians. For the first time in the history of their people, they had a fixed food supply which allowed them free time for other pursuits. Artwork increased both in quantity and in quality. A fixed food supply also led to a marked increase in population, to fixed settlements for certain groups, and to more complex social and cultural systems. No culture demonstrated this new vitality and complexity more dramatically than the Hopewell Culture.

The Hopewell Culture lasted for perhaps 600 years until about A.D. 700. The Hopewells were artisans and craftsmen who made fine jewelry, ornaments, and pottery. They maintained a network of trade routes which spanned most of the country. Their religion was complex and seemed to center around their mounds, the greatest number dotting the region along the Ohio Valley. What happened to the Hopewells remains a mystery, but their influence disappeared. The next few hundred years were characterized by a growing regional nationalism.

By the time the first European explorers reached the New World, the Northeast had become the home of numerous independent tribes. Along the Atlantic Coast lived a number of tribes belonging to the Algonquian language family. Inland, in a territory bounded by the Hudson River to the east and middle Ohio to the west, lived the powerful tribes of the Iroquoian language family. And west of them, Algonquians again resided in the area around the Great Lakes.

At the time of European contact, the Indians of the Northeast woodlands had certain characteristics in common. Most of the tribes lived in villages. They farmed to augment their food supply. Each tribe consisted of clans, which were composed of family groups; it was forbidden to marry within one's own clan. Clothing was manufactured from animal skins. Men wore a breechclout; women a wraparound skirt. During winter, both sexes wore moccasins, leggings, shirts, and robes. Honor played a vital role for Indian men, and the principal way of gaining honor was through acts of bravery in warfare, whether involving entire tribes or by valor shown in smaller raids on enemy villages. Religion was a major ingredient of Indian life, and though different spirits were worshipped by different tribes, there was a central belief in a Supreme Being. There were other similarities, of course, but there were also differences, differences which made the Algonquians and Iroquoians bitter enemies.

The Algonquians were the first Indians to welcome the Europeans. Their numbers were many and they occupied a territory extending from Labrador to the Hudson Bay with two prongs reaching southward. One prong stretched along the Atlantic seaboard from New Brunswick to Virginia. The other dipped down east of the Mississippi River and reached into Tennessee.

The Algonquians were hunters and as such lived and traveled lightly. They moved on foot, using snowshoes in the winter. They constructed lightweight canoes made primarily from birch bark. Their villages were often semi-permanent, enabling them to move quickly to new hunting grounds. They lived in easily erected, easily dismantled dwellings, the conical-shaped wigwam. Even their social structure, the loosely knit confederacies and the practice of breaking down tribal units into smaller, mobile hunting groups, reflected this concern for unencumberment and utility.

The Algonquian religion saw a strong relationship between the hunter and the hunted. A brotherhood existed between men and the creatures of the forest. All creatures were guarded by the supernatural, and man could kill another creature only from necessity. The hunted had to be treated with respect both before and after the kill, lest the dead's spirit return to haunt the hunter and his tribe.

Although most of the Algonquians practiced some farming, it assumed the greatest importance with the southern tribes. Farming was a woman's job. The man might clear the field for planting, but it was the woman's responsibility to tend and cultivate the crops. Corn was the chief crop. It was frequently supplemented with beans, pumpkins, wild rice, and other foods. The Algonquians also grew tobacco.

Periodically, a community of Algonquian tribes held pow-wows to discuss problems and reestablish ties. These gatherings, however, failed to establish any lasting intertribal unity. Politically, the Algonquian tribes were independent, behaving like tiny nations. They occasionally joined small confederacies, but these were usually highly informal and short-lived. Intertribal rivalry and feuding was a way of life among the Algonquians. When the white invaders came with their divine imperatives and superior weaponry, the Algonquians were unable to present a unified front against the invasion. Trapped between the greedy Europeans and the fierce Iroquoians, the Algonquian tribes along the Atlantic seaboard were virtually exterminated.

The Iroquoians had firmly established themselves in the Northeast by the middle of the fourteenth century. They were more sedentary and agricultural than were the Algonquians. They lived in fortified villages, secured most of their food through farming, and built sturdy lodges. Their dwellings, in fact, gave them their name—"people of the extended lodge," or "people of the longhouse." Despite their settled ways, they were implacable warriors and greatly feared in battle. They possessed another attribute—political sophistication.

Around 1570, five nations of the Iroquoians—the Seneca, the Cayuga, the Onondaga, the Oneida, and the Mohawk—agreed to join a league. As it turned out, the League of the Iroquois was a masterpiece of political planning. It created an Indian nation that dominated the Northeast and resisted for a time the overpowering white invasion. It probably even influenced the European colonists when they designed the Constitution of the United States.

The League of the Iroquois had two representative bodies,

and a third, moderating, branch. The first body was the Council of Chiefs. Its members, known as sachems, were elected by the women of the noble families in proportion to the size of each tribal unit. There were fifty sachems, and they served a term for life unless deposed by the women who had selected them. Members of the second body, the Pine Tree Chiefs, were chosen on the basis of merit, usually from among the famed warriors. The Firekeepers, made up of the chiefs of the Onondaga, served as the moderating body.

The League usually convened each summer to discuss problems of intertribal concern. (In this organization, each of the five tribes enjoyed local self-government and acted jointly in matters of common import.) Each tribe had one vote, and unanimous votes were required to reach decisions. In 1713 the Five Nations became the Six Nations when the council accepted the Tuscarorans, who had been driven from North Carolina by the colonists.

As the League served the common interests of the Five Nations, a similar political structure served the needs of each tribe. In local government three grades of leaders—representative of the judicial, legislative, and executive bodies—ran tribal affairs. As with the League, local leaders or chiefs were appointed by the women and were subject to their approval. This sturdiness and sophistication of political life reflected the same factors in Iroquoian life generally.

As mentioned, the Iroquois were known as the "people of the extended lodge." Their dwellings were long bark-covered structures, barrel-shaped like the U.S. Army's famed Quonset hut. Each dwelling housed as many as a dozen families. Iroquoian villages, or towns, were large and impressive and were usually surrounded by wooden stockades. Early explorers frequently referred to these towns as forts and castles.

At the hub of Iroquois life was the "fireside," the mother and her children. As in political matters, the women occupied a special position. Lineage was traced through her, and the most important male figure to an Iroquoian child was not his father but his mother's brother.

Religiously, the Iroquois believed in a number of powerful spirits. At the top of the spiritual hierarchy was the Master of Life, who represented the powers of good and had created the world. He was continually opposed by the powers of evil. Accordingly, each person in a tribe possessed an inner spiritual power which helped him combat the forces of evil.

The Iroquois were fierce warriors and their savagery in battle was legendary. The Algonquians called them "snakes" while the Delaware applied a special name *Mingwe,* meaning treacherous. With their fearful weapon the tomahawk the Iroquois were masters of the surprise attack. They frequently took prisoners and tortured them. If an enemy warrior stood up well under this torture, such as running the gauntlet, he might be adopted into the tribe. If not, he might be tortured to death and his body eaten by his captors.

When the Europeans came to the New World they established trade relations with the Iroquois, much of it in fur. By 1650 the Five Nations had depleted much of the beaver in their territory, and they launched a series of wars against other Iroquoian tribes, defeating the Huron, the Neutrals, the Erie, and the Susquehanna. During the French-English conflict the Five Nations allied themselves with the British, but during the American Revolution the Six Nations (it was after the Tuscarorans had joined the League) divided their allegiance, the Cayuga, Onondaga, Seneca, and Mohawk siding with the British and the Oneida and Tuscarora with the colonists. The outcome of this split, however, was not as devastating as might be expected, and today the Iroquois remain an important Indian group. Many Iroquois still consider themselves a separate nation and adhere to the old League.

What the final outcome of the enmity between the Algonquians and Iroquoians would have been remains academic. There was warfare, to be certain, but it was a warfare that was interrupted by a third party. Indian history was abruptly halted when the Europeans began colonizing the New World. For the most part the Indians of the Northeast succumbed to the waves of white-skinned Europeans.

INDIANS OF THE SOUTHEAST

How long ago men first wandered into the area of the Southeast is unknown. Ten thousand years ago is a safe estimate, though men were probably there long before then. Archaeologists confess that there are many, many sites they have been unable to get to yet. We do know that early man hunted Pleistocene mammals in the bogs and lowlands of the prehistoric Southeast at some time before these giant beasts died off. We know that these early bands of nomadic hunters used fluted points and spear throwers, which have been dated within the Paleo-Indian stage flourishing between 10,000 and 20,000 years ago. But as far as a reasonably precise date, or even an accurate surmisal of the routes these Paleo-Indians followed to arrive in the Southeast, we remain in the dark.

The sites and artifacts thus far uncovered tell us that the Southeast was the home of many populous tribes belonging to several different language families. There were representatives from the Muskogean, Tunican, Siouan, Iroquoian, and Algonquian language stocks. Culturally, the Southeast has a rich and important past, rivaling even that of the Southwest. Socially, these cultural traditions established caste lines which were similarly present in Aztec Mexico, Inca Peru, and Middle-Age Europe.

As the big-game animals died off, the prehistoric Indians turned increasingly to gathering vegetation and to small-game hunting. The comparatively mild climate of the Southeast and the abundance of natural food made survival easier here than in other parts of North America. Perhaps for this reason the early Indians in the Southeast were able to turn their attention to other matters. As early as 1700 B.C. a cultural tradition had begun. This was the Poverty Point Culture, which began along the lower Mississippi River and was probably the first in a succession of cultures which led to the dominance of agriculture, large concentrations of population, complex religious systems, and stratified social orders. These early cultural traditions resulted approximately 1,000 years later in a particularly vibrant culture developed along the bottomlands of the middle Mississippi River.

The Middle Mississippi Culture which emerged around A.D. 700 had its roots in numerous older cultures, especially the Hopewellian and Mexican traditions. It was characterized by large ceremonial centers containing one or several burial and temple mounds. The burial mounds were Hopewellian, though unmistakably smaller than the sprawling round-topped mounds dotting the Ohio Valley. The temple mounds were Mexican, flat-topped earthen pyramids with wooden temples on their summits. Together, these two types of mounds formed the square plazas of the ceremonial centers from where the rulers controlled satellite farming towns.

The Middle Mississippi Culture spread throughout the Southeast promoting the development of large metropolitan areas where the ceremonial center remained the hub of culture and civilization. Complex labor and social divisions undoubtedly existed and a new sophistication in artwork and pottery emerged. It was a "golden era" for the Indians of the Southeast.

Exactly how or why the temple-mound culture passed into obscurity around 1600 remains a question facing archaeologists today. Some postulate a death cult, a religious movement which diverted the Middle Mississippians from further progress and actually led to a deterioration of their culture. Others blame the waves of diseases which swept the New World after European contact. Whatever the reason, the culture faded, leaving a remnant dwelling along the lower Mississippi River.

When the white man came to the Southeast he found a number of tribes living in the region which had once supported the Middle Mississippians. Most of these tribes had no temple-mound traditions, but a few had retained some elements of their past, the most notable being the Natchez Indians, who occupied a number of towns in the area of the present Natchez, Mississippi.

The Natchez were some 4,000 strong when the French first came into this area, and they lived in a way that experts feel resembled the old culture. They were ruled by a despot called the Great Sun. He had absolute power and was believed to have descended from the sun. His relatives belonged to the Sun Clan and were known as Little Suns. They constituted the ruling class. Immediately beneath them were the Nobles. Honored Men came next, and finally came the class of commoners known as Stinkards.

Natchez society functioned along these class lines, but there was one unusual feature. Suns were required to mate from the Stinkard class. And since class status followed the female line of descent, a child born of a Sun mother and Stinkard father became a Sun. Yet, a child born to a Stinkard mother and Sun father would not be relegated to the Stinkard class. Out of deference to his father's position he would be a Noble. Most Stinkards—and they were in the great majority—married other Stinkards, though, and their children were also Stinkards.

Natchez society was also characterized by elaborate religious practices. They were sun worshippers, and Natchez life revolved around this worship, which revolved around the politico-religious leaders.

The Natchez were a sedentary people and like the old culture placed great emphasis on agriculture. But when the French came, their days of agriculture and their days of sun worship came to an abrupt end. In 1729 the French tried to take control of one of the Natchez towns to use as a plantation. The Natchez revolted and attacked a French force at Fort Rosalie. But this attack merely led to strong countermeasures by the French, and by 1730 the Natchez as a tribal unit had been destroyed.

The coming of the white man proved disastrous for other Indian groups of the Southeast as well. Although there were several language families dwelling in this region, two deserve special mention—the Muskogeans and the Siouans.

Tribes of the Muskogean language family occupied the Gulf States, including nearly all of Mississippi and Alabama and parts of Tennessee, Georgia, and South Carolina. The best known of these tribes were the Chickasaw, Choctaw, and Creeks, who together with the Iroquoian-speaking Cherokee and an offshoot of the Creek Confederacy, the Seminole, formed what is known as the Five Civilized Nations—so called because of the ease with which they adapted to the white man's culture.

The Muskogeans were an agricultural and sedentary people. Politically, they were advanced, as shown by the Creek Confederacy which extended throughout Alabama and Georgia. This confederacy permitted each member tribe a large degree of autonomy while providing a strong, collective defensive system. The confederacy itself was composed of approximately fifty towns divided into two classes. White—or peace—towns dealt with matters of civil government; Red—or war—towns handled military affairs.

European contact came around 1528 when Panfilo de Narvaez met the Apalachee of western Florida. Around 1540,

Hernando De Soto explored the entire Muskogean territory while searching for a civilization which would rival that of the Incas. From that point, European contact increased. English, French, and Spanish settlements began exerting new pressures on the Muskogeans, gradually pushing them back from the Atlantic and Gulf regions. By 1840 the Muskogeans had been removed from the Southeast with the exception of a few hundred Seminole in Florida and pockets of Choctaw in Mississippi, Alabama, and Louisiana.

The Siouan tribes at one time made up one of the largest linguistic groups in North America. Most people are familiar with the Siouans who lived in the Midwest and Plains states, but few are aware of those who had once lived in the Southeast.

When the first Europeans landed in the New World, the Southeastern Siouans had a past tradition of strength and glory. They had once commanded the territory from Florida to West Virginia, but they had reached their peak and were on a rapid decline. The Algonquians and Iroquoians to the north, and Muskogeans to the south and west were already making inroads into the region occupied by more than two dozen Siouan tribes, a region comprising the present states of West Virginia, Virginia, North Carolina, and South Carolina.

The story of the Southeastern Siouans—which includes a scattering of tribes such as the Biloxi and Mosopelea outside of this four-state area—is one shrouded with mystery and tragedy, the tale of a people who after rising to power spiraled rapidly downward to virtual extinction. Where they came from, these people who were agricultural, practiced head-flattening and tattooing, and wore their hair long, remains unanswered. When they came is another question puzzling scientists. What we know is restricted to the historical period after European chroniclers had arrived in the New World.

And the story these chroniclers tell is one filled with sorrow, the story of incessant attacks by hostile tribes, of alcoholism and dehumanization, of disease, of flight and incorporation into larger tribes, and finally of extinction. Within the larger story were numerous smaller tales of tribes like the Congaree, who lost more than half their people to white slave traders; or the Sewee, who were practically wiped out by disease and alcohol; or even the Sugaree, who disappeared, victims of warfare. In all, the Southeastern Siouans left little behind—a few notes in scattered journals, a few cities named after their tribes, and a few geographical sites of interest. The bloodline which they so highly valued was wasted, spilled on the battlefield, dried into dust in lonely graves, and dispersed with the blood-lines of other Indians from other language families.

INDIANS OF THE CENTRAL WOODLANDS AND PRAIRIES

Indians moved into the central prairies and woodlands soon after the Ice Age. This area was well stocked with game, and the soil was rich and supported an abundance of natural foods. As populations grew, a succession of cultures—including the first metalworkers (Old Copper Culture), the mound builders (Adena and Hopewell), and the temple-mound builders (Middle Missis-sippi)—emerged and passed away. By historic times, the area had become populated largely by two language groups: the Algonquians and the Siouans.

The Algonquians occupied a larger portion of North Amer-ica than any other language group. In the central region their life-style resembled that of their kindred along the Atlantic Coast. Agriculture was important, with maize, beans, squash, and tobacco being principal crops. Hunting, too, was an impor-tant source of food, and tribes like the Kickapoo and Chippewa regularly ventured out to the Plains to hunt buffalo. Although many of the Algonquian tribes of this region lived a mobile existence, a few tribes lived in fixed villages. In general, tribes foraged over large areas of land and came together once or twice a year for a festival in the central village. In religion, great respect was paid to a myriad of objects and deities, including the sun, moon, trees, various animals, and the four cardinal points. They believed in a cosmic substance prevailing through-out nature, and persons or objects imbued with it were held in special veneration.

The Siouans of this region were part agriculturists and part hunters. Many accounts from early European explorers praise the maize fields of such Siouan tribes as the Quapaw and the Iowa. The land was fertile, and this contributed to a life-style more sedentary than that of their western brothers on the Plains. The Siouans of the woodlands and prairies lived in fixed villages and usually resided in large earthen dwellings. Like many of the central Algonquians, they made periodic forays onto the Plains to hunt buffalo. And the Siouans were deeply religious, believing in a mystical transcendentalism, a cosmic interrelationship between Creator and Created. They regarded the world around them with respect and felt deeply involved in and responsible for that world. But these were not traits of just the Siouans or Algonquians. The Indians of the central prairies and woodlands reflected many of the elements of the American Indian as a whole.

As the English frontier advanced in the East, surviving Algonquian tribes fled westward into the Ohio and Mississippi valleys. There, they met and allied themselves with the French, who still held the territory west of the Appalachians. The Northwest Territory became a melting pot of such Algonquian tribes as the Miami, Kickapoo, Potawatomi, Shawnee, Sauk, Fox, Chippewa, Illinois, Delaware, and Ottawa; and these tribes, together with a handful of French soldiers, formed a wall of resistance against the advancing English frontier.

For several years, the Indians of the old Northwest enjoyed a degree of security. This was soon to change, however. With the defeat of the French in the French and Indian War, 1754-63, the English claimed ownership of the territory east of the Mississippi River. And English soldiers replaced French garrisons at the series of forts running from Mackinaw to Pittsburgh.

The fall of the French spurred a new wave of white settlement west of the Appalachians. Alarmed by this and by the stern British policy toward the Indians, Chief Pontiac of the Ottawas urged the Algonquians along the frontier to attack the English. In the spring of 1763 he laid siege to the fort at Detroit and signalled an uprising which took every major fort from Michigan to Pennsylvania except, ironically, Detroit itself and also Pittsburgh. These two forts—Fort Pitt and Fort Detroit—were to prove Pontiac's undoing. Failing to capture them, he lost his Indian and French supporters and was forced to sue for peace.

Several years later, in 1794, an army sent by the newly formed Republic of the United States penetrated eastern Ohio on a mission to destroy Indian resistance to the expanding white frontier. This army, headed by General Anthony ("Mad Anthony") Wayne, met and engaged an Algonquian force near the present Maumee, Ohio. The ensuing battle, the Battle of Fallen Timbers, led to the loss of most of Ohio and part of Indiana.

After Fallen Timbers a Shawnee warrior who had participated in the battle traveled from tribe to tribe in order to create a united Indian front to block further white encroachment. His name was Tecumseh, and together with his brother, who was known simply as The Prophet, he managed to amalgamate several tribes. But before his confederacy reached maturity, General William Henry Harrison led an attack against Prophet Town, the confederacy's center, located near the mouth of the Tippecanoe River in northern Indiana. Tecumseh's strength was destroyed, and he withdrew into Canada and subsequently joined with the British in the War of 1812.

The War of 1812 left Indian strength east of the Mississippi considerably weakened. Settlers poured westward and tribe after tribe was forced to cross the Mississippi. One Indian chieftain refused to leave his homeland in the Rock River valley in northern Illinois. Black Hawk, a Sauk war chief, had grown incensed with the white man's injustice. One incident in particular infuriated him. In 1804, General Harrison had invited a Sauk hunting party into the fort at St. Louis. There he plied them with liquor and tricked them into selling all the Sauk land in Illinois. The Treaty of 1804 was a farce, but many of the Sauk Indians complied and moved into Iowa. Black Hawk was indignant. For years after the treaty he berated Keokuk, a prominent councilman who had passively played into the white government's hands by urging the move, and he adamantly refused to accept the treaty as valid.

During the War of 1812, Black Hawk fought with Tecumseh and the British against the Americans. After the war, he returned to his home along the Rock River. He then launched a lonely crusade to muster support from other tribes and the British to help him fight the treaty, but by 1830 white settlers had moved into his homeland.

The Spring of 1832 saw the situation come to a head. In April, Black Hawk and several hundred of his people returned to the valley after the winter's hunting time. The Indians conducted themselves peacefully and told the white settlers in the valley that they had returned only to grow corn. But the settlers panicked and sent to Washington for army protection. The army, headed by General Henry Atkinson, arrived and took the offensive, capturing three warriors who had been sent under a flag of truce to talk with the army. A battle erupted and Black Hawk led a skillful retreat into Wisconsin. There he was chased by Atkinson and managed to elude him several times. But for Black Hawk, as for the other Indians east of the Mississippi, history had run out. The white man had become too many and too strong. The end came in August near the mouth of the Bad Axe River. Black Hawk and his people were trapped between a warship which had been positioned on the Mississippi and General Atkinson's army. The chief made a feeble stand, but the battle turned into a massacre as American sharpshooters picked off Indian men, women, and children who had been driven into the water. Black Hawk himself managed to escape but surrendered a few days later. The last Indian leader of the old Northwest had been defeated, and the Indian lands east of the Mississippi belonged to the white man.

INDIANS OF THE PLAINS

The Great Plains is a geographical area stretching roughly from the Mississippi River to the Rocky Mountains and extending well into Canada northward and Texas southward. It is composed of two varying regions. In the eastern half the rainfall averages from twenty to forty inches per year, yielding the tall-grass prairieland. The western half receives less than twenty inches of rain a year and is relatively barren of trees and dominated by short, drought-resistant grasses. Ten thousand years ago this entire region presented a different face. Then, as Folsom Man followed the game trails of the giant Ice Age mammals, the Plains were a land of lakes and forests and abundant rainfall.

Archaeologists have asserted that man has lived on the Plains for at least 11,000 years. Trails of projectile points and stone and bone implements reveal that small nomadic bands of people hunted the mammoth, the giant ground sloth, and the big-horned bison. When the Ice Age ended, the Plains gradually grew hotter and drier. With the change in climate and ecology, the game animals and their hunters steadily withdrew. About 5,000 years ago, the Plains reached a peak of heat and aridity. The people who were left in this region became gatherers and small-game hunters, using every resource available to them for survival.

As time approached the Christian era, influences from the mound builders to the east reached outward to the Plains. Pockets of settlements scattered from the Mississippi to the Rockies became semi-permanent, used burial mounds, practiced pottery-making, and developed agriculture. Much of this activity occurred in the eastern portion of the Plains, leaving behind several Hopewellian sites in the Prairie States.

Approximately a thousand years ago, this cultural activity increased. Groups of Indians influenced by the Mississippian Culture began a slow migration into the Plains. They developed strong agricultural economies along watercourses and used hunters who roamed as far as the Rocky Mountains to augment their farm crops.

As the Pre-Columbian era drew to an end, many of the more westerly communities had already been abandoned, their residents returning to the nomadic hunting and gathering ways of their ancestors. By the time the first white expedition into the Plains left Mexico in 1540—Coronado's search for the Seven Cities of Cibola—the Plains Indians represented two distinct cultures. One occupied the eastern portion of the Plains. They lived in more or less permanent villages and based much of their economy on agriculture. The other resided largely in the western portion. These Indians were nomadic and relied primarily on the buffalo for food, shelter, and clothing.

The entrance of the white man into the Plains had a great impact upon the life-styles of these two groups of Indians. The most dramatic of these changes was the introduction of the horse, which within the space of a comparatively few years, radically altered centuries-old patterns.

The horse offered several significant advantages to the Indians. It became a measure of wealth and a symbol of a man's status within a tribe. It made hunting easier. The mounted hunter could cover great distances fast. The horse could be used as a beast of burden, enabling nomadic tribes to transport greater amounts of supplies easier and faster. And as a weapon in warfare, the horse gave a formidable advantage. Indians were able to swoop down in lightning raids, an advantage equalled only by the introduction of the gun.

After its introduction by the Spaniards in Mexico late in the sixteenth century, the horse quickly spread from tribe to tribe. Sedentary tribes in the eastern Plains region like the Omaha, Dakota, Ponca, and Oto recognized its value as an important tool enhancing their chances of survival. In the northwestern region of the Plains the Algonquian-speaking Blackfoot Confederacy became horse-riding, nomadic buffalo hunters. Meanwhile, eastern pressures were gradually forcing Indians westward. The Plains, like the old Northwest Territory, was becoming a melting pot of various Indian groups who readily adapted to the buffalo-hunting culture. By the beginning of the nineteenth century, the Plains Culture had emerged and the era of the portable tipi, the war bonnet, and the swift raid by horseback was in full swing.

For a brief time, the Plains region eluded the frontier pressure which had devastated Indian life east of the Mississippi. In place of the Indian-white tension which had characterized the East, Indian-Indian tension characterized the Plains. Intertribal raiding became a way of life, and a new value system sprouted around war activities. The horse raid supplanted other activities in importance, and a warrior could claim little status until he had acquired horses and proven his bravery in warfare. New war societies emerged among the Plains Indians and warriors derived prestige from belonging to them. On the battlefield a code of behavior developed in which certain feats bestowed great honor on a warrior. For example, counting coup on a live enemy (touching him with a special stick) was considered very dangerous and thus was a highly valued act. When a warrior who had counted coup returned to camp, he would boast of his deeds, and others would hold him in esteem.

All of this was an art, of course, and certain tribes took greater interest in the art of warfare. In the northern Plains the Sioux, who had abandoned their agricultural-based villages along the Plains' eastern fringe, vigorously developed their skills in horsemanship and warfare. By the mid-1800's they controlled a large area extending over the states of North and

South Dakota and parts of Wyoming and Nebraska. In the southern Plains the Comanche rose to dominance.

The Sioux and the Comanche—indeed, all the Indians of the Plains—were ill-fated, however. When the white man finally turned his attention to the West, it required only forty years to accomplish what had taken him 300 years to do in the East. The plunder of the West began in 1849, when gold was discovered in California. It ended on the morning of December 29, 1890, when the 7th U.S. Cavalry massacred over 200 Indian men, women, and children at Wounded Knee Creek in South Dakota.

INDIANS OF THE PLATEAU AND THE GREAT BASIN

The Plateau region of the Northwest stretches from the Rocky Mountains to the Cascade Range and from southern Canada to northern Nevada. It is a land characterized by rushing streams, river basins, wind-swept plateaus, canyons, and forested mountainsides. The mighty Columbia River is born in this region and is fed by a host of rivers and streams as it snakes its way to the Pacific Ocean.

People have occupied the Plateau region for at least 11,000 years. Scientists have determined that the first permanent inhabitants of the Plateau in all probability belonged to a particular cultural group which used a double-pointed, leaf-shaped spear point. They have classified this group as the Old Cordilleran Culture.

The Old Cordilleran Culture was a hunting, fishing, and gathering culture. It prevailed for thousands of years, eventually absorbing traits of other cultures. By approximately 8,000 years ago, nomadic bands had pushed from the protection of the mountains into the interior of the Plateau. At about the same time, influences from the gathering-economy Indians in the Great Basin to the south crept northward. Basketry appeared and also the milling stone, both of which typified the Great Basin's Desert Culture. As influences also crept into the Plateau from the north a Plateau Culture emerged.

By the time white men ventured into the Plateau region, the Indians there lived in villages along the major rivers and tributaries. They relied greatly on river travel for transportation. The basis of their economy was fishing and salmon was the main staple. They had no agriculture, but supplemented their diet with roots (especially camas), berries, and small game. Towards the Cascade Range in eastern Washington and Oregon a few Indian groups practiced head-flattening and pierced their noses. On the Rocky Mountain side, a few tribes incorporated elements of the Plains Culture, making regular excursions into the Plains to hunt buffalo and using the buffalo in ways characteristic of the Plains Indians.

The Great Basin emerges south of the Plateau. It is an arid and seemingly uninhabitable region, but Indians have lived there for nearly as long as they have lived in the Plateau. The economy of these Basin Indians is based on gathering.

Much about the early Basin Indians remains a mystery. The region itself—which encompasses the land between the Rocky Mountains to the east, the Sierra Nevada Mountains to the west, southern Idaho to the north, and northern Arizona to the south—is desert and thwarts human exploration. But despite this and other problems, archaeologists have still managed to garner a few details about the early Basin dwellers.

Around 11,000 years ago the Great Basin was probably inhabited by thinly scattered bands of big-game hunters. In the western portion there lived a few bands of hunters and gatherers belonging to the Old Cordilleran Culture. Over the next 2000 years the population increased somewhat, and a culture based almost solely on food-gathering emerged. There was no agriculture. The Indians were nomadic and followed seasonal routes where they gathered or caught anything edible. They hunted deer and antelope, practically luxuries in this harsh climate. They gathered seeds, berries, nuts, and roots, and trapped grasshoppers, lizards, rabbits, mice, and small birds. The Basin Indians usually lived in small, extended family units. Though there was little tribal unity, several family units might join together during the winter at special winter villages where water and fuel were available.

Because of the barrenness of the terrain, almost all human energy went into survival; thus very little cultural development occurred, and this desert culture persisted practically unchanged for thousands of years. The Indians of the Great Basin have often been classified as the most primitive of the American

Indians. Whites have ridiculed them and have contemptuously called them "diggers." When the white man finally entered the Basin region, he found the Indians there easy to subdue, and he did subdue them, placing them on reservations with little regard for their welfare. Today the Indians of the Great Basin are among the poorest. But they were not the only Indians to suffer at the hands of white men. The Plateau Indians, too, saw their land taken, their women and children murdered. And perhaps no group better exemplifies the fate of the Plateau and Basin Indians at the hands of the white conquerors than do the Nez Perce.

The Nez Perce (pierced noses) lived in Idaho, Oregon, and Washington. Contrary to their name, it is not known that they practiced the art of nose piercing. The French gave them this name, possibly because their tribal designation in sign language implied such. In 1855 they were assigned a reservation which included portions of Oregon and Idaho. When gold was discovered in the Oregon Territory, a flood of miners invaded their lands. The government then appropriated their Oregon holdings and ordered the Nez Perce to remove to Idaho. One group of the Nez Perce, under a powerful leader called Chief Joseph by the whites, refused. In May, 1877, General Oliver Otis Howard summoned Joseph to a council at Fort Lapwai. At the conclusion of their meeting, Howard gave the Nez Perce of the Wallowa Valley an ultimatum: if they had not removed within thirty days, the soldiers would remove them.

A sad and angry Joseph returned to his village. Realizing that his people would stand little chance against the might of the white army, he decided to move his village to the buffalo country of Montana and ordered them across the Snake River. But during the crossing, a group of white rustlers stole some of their livestock. The Indians were rightfully angry at the incident and a few young, hotheaded warriors retaliated by killing eleven whites. From that point there was no turning back.

On the morning of June 17, 1877, two companies of soldiers under the command of Captain David Perry attempted to launch a surprise attack on Joseph's temporary encampment in Idaho's Lahmotta Canyon. Joseph, forewarned, was ready, and although heavily outnumbered, soundly defeated Perry's force. Joseph now abandoned any hope of settling in Montana.

He knew the soldiers would be after him and the only hope of his people would be to reach Canada.

He conducted a masterful retreat across the Bitterroot Mountains into Montana with General Howard's army relentlessly pursuing them from behind. From the east, Colonel John Gibbon with a large force attempted to cut him off.

On the morning of August 10, Gibbon attacked the sleeping Nez Perce camp on the Big Hole River, but Joseph managed to turn the attack and lead his people to safety. In the foray, however, he lost eighty of his people, mostly women and children. By the time the Nez Perce had reached Yellowstone Park, the U.S. Army's 7th Cavalry had been added to the chase. And, after a summer and autumn of grueling flight, the Indians were finally trapped early in November. The Cavalry, under command of Colonel Bear Coat Miles, cut off their retreat just one day's march from the Canadian border.

Joseph and his followers were removed to Indian Territory, where disease took a frightening toll. The Nez Perce were finally moved to a reservation in northern Washington.

INDIANS OF THE SOUTHWEST

South of the Great Basin lies an area which seems forgotten in nature's scheme of things. Rising from low, cactus-studded desert in the south, through a mountainous region of bare, rugged peaks scarred by deep valleys, to high plateau in the north, the Southwest is both hot and dry. For the present-day inhabitants of the Southwest (which includes Arizona and parts of New Mexico, Utah, Colorado, and Texas), as well as for the Indians whose ancestors have lived in this region since the days of Folsom Man, and probably earlier, water is a commodity both precious and scarce. Rainfall is slight, evaporation is high, and though fed by three major river systems, the Colorado, the Gila, and the Rio Grande, the region nevertheless remains arid.

Despite the harsh land, the region did not remain unpeopled. And unlike the Indians of the Great Basin, the Indians of the Southwest did not remain primitive gatherers.

It is not known when man first entered the Southwest. Findings at Sandia Cave in New Mexico suggest human occupancy 20,000 years ago, but these findings have not been accepted in all scientific circles. But man was here at least 10,000 years ago. Whatever the date, the earliest men were big-game hunters who left a trail of projectile points and stone implements behind.

With the end of the Ice Age and the extinction of the big-game mammals, the people of the Southwest turned to gathering. Along the shores of a now-extinct lake, these gatherers learned to use milling stones to grind seeds and nuts. Archaeologists believe that these prehistoric dwellers along the ancient Lake Cochise were among the first Indians to develop the food-gathering Desert Culture. They, like the Indians of the Great Basin, used everything edible. They were seminomadic and lived in temporary camps along the lakes and streams which once characterized the Southwest and have since dried up.

The Cochise Culture lasted for several thousand years. Through a succession of stages as climatic changes slowly altered the face of the land, Cochise gatherers lived off a dwindling supply of natural resources. As the Southwest grew hotter and drier, the Cochise people continually had to alter their diet as more and more species withered away. They slept in caves, rock overhangs, and portable wickiups and wore clothing manufactured from animal skins and woven vegetable fibers. Despite these changes, and despite the ever-present need to range more widely for food, the Cochise people changed little for nearly nine millenniums. Then, near the beginning of the Christian era, the Cochise Culture yielded to the birth of two daughter cultures.

The first of these cultures, the Mogollon, sprouted in the southern corners of Arizona and New Mexico. It was based on a gathering economy, which persisted for another thousand years, but the Mogollons also raised some of their own crops. They made undecorated pottery and lived in pit houses. The second culture, the Hohokam, emerged in the desert lands of central and southern Arizona.

Like its sister culture, the Hohokam engaged in agriculture, produced pottery, and lived in pit houses. But the Hohokam advanced at a faster rate, developing technology and art forms new to the region. Among the more significant of these developments were the irrigation works and canal networks which enabled the Hohokams to cultivate thousands of acres of land.

In addition, the Hohokams constructed earthen pyramids and fashioned clay figurines, both showing a strong influence from Mexico.

To the north of the Hohokam and the Mogollon, approximately where the four corners of Utah, Colorado, Arizona, and New Mexico meet, a third cultural group, the Anasazi, was emerging. The Anasazi followed the traditional sequence, passing from a gathering to an agricultural economy. By A.D. 400, they had adopted the pit-house dwelling. By A.D. 800, they were constructing their dwellings above ground. They used stone and adobe and built their houses in clusters. By 1250, the Anasazi had constructed a number of communal settlements, some of their buildings reaching four and five stories high and containing as many as 800 rooms (the likes of which can be seen today in Mesa Verde National Park in Colorado and in Chaco Canyon in New Mexico). They developed pottery-making to a fine degree, their work showing a flair for design. They manufactured colorful blankets, turquoise jewelry, and ornamental sandals and clothing. They practiced dry-land farming, growing maize, squash, beans, cotton, and tobacco.

As the Anasazi culture reached its peak, it influenced the cultures to the south. The Hohokam and Mogollon cultures began showing marked Anasazi influences. Clusters of multi-roomed pueblos and pottery with geometric designs appeared. Around 1100, the Mogollon Culture became essentially that of the Anasazi, while the Hohokam Culture retained a degree of autonomy. Then, as the thirteenth century waned, these three cultures entered a period of decline.

Some authorities blame this decline on a twenty-three-year drought which tree-ring dating reveals hit the Southwest from 1276 to 1299. The Anasazi abandoned their dwellings, and together with many of the Pueblo Culture people of the Hohokam-Mogollon, moved southward to the Rio Grande and into Mexico. They were undoubtedly prompted on their way by the increased activity of nomadic bands from Canada, the fierce Apache and Navajo who had been migrating into the Southwest since A.D. 1000.

By the time the Spaniards entered the Southwest, the great Hohokam-Mogollon and Anasazi cultures had died. Their descendants, however, the Zuni, Hopi, Pueblos, and others, retained many of the old ways. They lived in stone and adobe pueblos, subsisted primarily from the labors of agriculture, made excellent pottery, and were exquisite weavers. These pueblo communities were strong social units based on cooperation. Concepts like individualism, competition, and aggression were considered offensive. Religion provided the cohesive force for this solidarity and permeated the lives of these pueblo dwellers. They were a peaceful people, but when threatened they could fight fiercely. In 1680, for example, the Pueblos of the Southwest united under Pope, a Tewa shaman, and drove the Spaniards from their communities in New Mexico.

Eventually, the Pueblos succumbed to the white invasion, but rather than continue a pattern of military aggression as the Apache had, they elected to follow a path of peaceful resistance. They admitted the white invasion, but they held on to their cultural traditions, screening out as much of the white influence as they could. And as other tribes were decimated by the white armies, the Pueblos lived on into the twentieth century, and even today uphold many of the old traditions.

INDIANS OF THE PACIFIC COAST

Along that stretch of Pacific coast which includes the present states of California, Oregon, and Washington, a true multiplicity of tribes, cultures, and languages existed. More than a hundred distinct tribes lived in the coastal region and represented cultural groupings ranging from the sophisticated, prestige-seeking Northwest Pacific Coast Culture to the primitive, austere Desert Culture. Ethnologists frequently refer to this geographic region as the "Tower of Babel," for more languages and dialects prevailed in this region than perhaps in any comparable region in the world.

When prehistoric man first entered this region remains unknown. Recent studies in San Bernardino County, California, indicate that he may have been there for at least 50,000 years, but that is an answer for the future. For the present, scientists have only a scanty picture of the prehistory of this region.

CALIFORNIA. Today, California is the most populous state in the Union. It is a state of complexities and contrasts, of varied groups of people from numerous ethnic and racial backgrounds. Present-day California thus reflects its past, for at one time California held the largest and most varied concentration of Indians in the land which would later become the United States.

As mentioned, evidence has been uncovered suggesting that California was inhabited at least 50,000 years ago. Other findings also indicate a great antiquity for man in this region. On Santa Rosa Island, the remains of dwarf mammoth which appear to have been butchered and roasted suggest an age of 30,000 years ago. Near La Jolla, artifacts have been found which may be 20,000 years old. But these dates have not yet been accepted by all scientists in the field, and it is generally assumed that by at least 9,000 years ago California was populated by big-game hunters.

As the big-game tradition passed, it was replaced by a gathering culture, and by 1,500 years ago the population of this natural paradise had already begun to evolve into differing cultures. Although the peoples of the desert region of southern California retained their gathering culture, the Indians along the coast turned increasingly to hunting, both on land and sea, and to the use of acorns as a primary source of food. Northward, the Indians of central and north California were beginning to feel the influence of the Northwest Pacific Coast Indians. They were beginning to build wooden dwellings and were venturing further out to sea to fish and to hunt sea mammals. Meanwhile, populations continued to increase and wandering bands of migratory Indians continued to enter California and stay.

By the time the Spaniards entered California, the Indians had established themselves in permanent locations within specific boundaries. The acorn had become the principal food staple, rendering agriculture unnecessary, and only one group of California Indians practiced farming, the Yuma along the Colorado River. In general, the California Indian lived a settled life. Most were peaceful. The mild climate permitted simple dress, the men often going naked, and the abundance of natural food freed many groups from the time-demanding chore of securing enough for survival. The Indians became excellent craftsmen. The basketry of the Hupa and Pomo Indians is said to have been among the finest in the world. They also had the time to develop complex social customs and a rich ceremonial life. Puberty rituals were common and festivals several times a year told and retold stories of creation. To the south, the Indians fashioned sleek canoes and lived in grass and reed huts. To the north, their dwellings grew sturdier, as tribes like the Shasta, Yurok, and Hupa constructed wooden houses from cedar planks. Inland, a few Shoshonean groups retained their gathering culture; for them life remained a struggle.

The Spaniards explored California during the sixteenth century. They established missions and outposts, and many of these early explorers considered the California Indians primitive because they were simple and non-aggressive. Sadly, it was these very qualities which led to the destruction of the California Indian population. They were easy prey for the ambitious and greedy whites who flooded California during the Gold Rush of 1849.

THE NORTHWEST PACIFIC COAST. The Northwest Pacific Coast stretches from Alaska's Prince William Sound to northern California. Along that coastline a narrow strip of land separates the coastal mountains from the Pacific Ocean. Unique in its climate, this coastal strip is warmed by the Japan Current and year round provides a region especially suited for a rich, full life. For this reason, and because of the great abundance of natural food from the sea, coastal rivers, and forests, the Indians of this region developed a vigorous culture, both highly advanced and complex.

Much about the prehistory of these Indians remains obscured. It is known that bands of hunters occupied this region about 8,000 years ago, but how they arrived there, their actual path of migration, remains a mystery. It is possible these early hunters followed river courses like that of the Columbia. Whatever their migratory route, however, by about 3,000 years ago the descendants of these hunters were turning to sea creatures for food. Around the beginning of the Christian era this transition was completed and the Indians of the coast were primarily sea-oriented, basing their economies on fishing and related activities.

By the time the white man came to the New World, the Indians of this region were culturally advanced. Prestige was the cornerstone of their life and individuals went to great lengths to achieve this prestige. The owning and giving away of property was the chief way of attaining status among one's peers. Periodically, usually to celebrate important events or atone for a loss of status, a property owner would hold a feast. An event of this sort was called a potlatch, and it was designed to show a man's greatness, wealth, and generosity. During a potlatch the host would make a great show of giving his wealth away to his guests. Sometimes he destroyed pieces of his wealth before them, all the while boasting of his greatness. In the end, the more wealth he could rid himself of—which included not only such things as blankets, copper, and canoes, but also human slaves—the greater his prestige.

Warfare was also an important activity for many of the coastal tribes. Warriors wore helmets and slat armor and frequently raided other tribes to procure slaves. Transportation for many of these raids was over water, for the coastal Indians were excellent canoe builders and sometimes fashioned crafts up to sixty feet in length.

After the white man came to this region the natural artistry of the Indians flourished. Always competent woodworkers, the coastal people were able to extend this artistry after receiving iron tools. One of the most impressive of these developments was the totem pole, which chronicled the personal history of the maker or the man who had commissioned the pole.

The first whites to reach the Northwest Pacific Coast were Russian fur traders. After them came Spanish, English, and American traders; and while the initial contact led to a cultural flowering, prolonged contact led to the ultimate destruction of the coastal Indians. Disease, whiskey, a few military clashes, and the collision of two different cultures caused the old ways to topple. And although a few villages still exist in British Columbia and a few woodcarvers still fashion totem poles, the glory of the era of the potlatch and totem pole is gone.

Bibliography

PART ONE. BLACK POWER: THE BLACK EXPERIENCE IN AMERICA

Books

Adams, Russell L. *Great Negroes Past and Present.* Chicago, 1964.

Alexis, Stephen. *Black Liberator.* New York, 1949.

Aptheker, Herbert. *American Negro Slave Revolts.* New York, 1943.

——. *A Documentary History of the Negro People in the United States.* New York, 1951.

Baldwin, James. *Notes of a Native Son.* Boston, 1955.

Barbour, Floyd B. (ed). *The Black Power Revolt.* New York, 1968.

Bardolph, Richard. *The Negro Vanguard.* New York, 1959.

Barron, Milton L. (ed). *American Minorities.* New York, 1957.

Belfrage, Sally. *Freedom Summer.* New York, 1965.

Bennett, Lerone, Jr. *Before the Mayflower: A History of the Negro in America, 1619-1964.* Baltimore, 1961.

——. *Negro Mood.* New York, 1965.

——. *What Manner of Man: A Biography of Martin Luther King, Jr.* New York, 1964.

Bleiweiss, Robert M. (ed). *Marching to Freedom: The Life of Martin Luther King, Jr.* Middletown, 1968.

Boas, Franz. *Race and Democratic Society.* New York, 1945.

Booker, Simeon. *Black Man's America.* Englewood Cliffs, 1964.

Breitman, George (ed). *Malcolm X Speaks.* New York, 1965.

Brink, William J. *The Negro Revolution in America.* New York, 1964.

Brown, H. Rap. *Die, Nigger, Die!* New York, 1969.

Buckmaster, Henrietta. *Let My People Go.* New York, 1941.

Carmichael, Stokely, and Charles V. Hamilton. *Black Power: The Politics of Liberation in America.* New York, 1967.

Cash, Wilbur J. *The Mind of the South.* New York, 1941.

Catton, Bruce. *The Coming Fury.* Garden City, 1961.

Chambers, Bradford (ed). *Chronicles of Black Protest.* New York, 1968.

Clark, Kenneth B. *Dark Ghetto: Dilemmas of Social Power.* New York, 1965.

Cleaver, Eldridge. *Soul on Ice.* New York, 1968.

Cohen, Jerry, and William S. Murphy. *Burn, Baby, Burn.* New York, 1966.

Cole, Ernest. *House of Bondage.* New York, 1967.

Conant, James Bryant. *Slums and Suburbs.* New York, 1961.

Conot, Robert. *Rivers of Blood, Years of Darkness.* New York, 1967.

Davidson, Basil. *Black Mother.* Boston, 1961.

Douglas, Frederick. *The Life and Times of Frederick Douglas.* Hartford, 1881.

Drake, St. Clair, and Horace R. Cayton. *Black Metropolis.* New York, 1945.

DuBois, W.E.B. *Black Folk: Then and Now.* New York, 1939.

——. *Dusk of Dawn.* New York, 1940.

——. *The Souls of Black Folk.* Chicago, 1903.

Durham, Philip, and Everett L. Jones. *The Negro Cowboys.* New York, 1965.

Eppse, Merl R. *The Negro, Too, in American History.* Chicago, 1939.

Essien-Udom, E.U. *Black Nationalism: A Search for an Identity in America.* New York, 1962.

Fanon, Frantz. *Black Skin, White Masks.* Translated by Charles Lam Markmann. New York, 1967.

——. *The Wretched of the Earth.* Translated by Constance Farrington. New York, 1966.

Farmer, James. *Freedom—When?* New York, 1965.

Fishman, Leo. *Poverty Amid Affluence.* New Haven, 1966.

Franklin, John Hope. *From Slavery to Freedom.* New York, 1947.

Frazier, E. Franklin. *Black Bourgeoisie.* Glencoe, 1957.

——. *The Negro in the United States.* New York, 1957.

——. *Race and Culture Contacts in the Modern World.* Boston, 1957.

Fulks, Bryan. *Black Struggle: A History of the Negro in America.* New York, 1969.

Galbraith, John K. *The Affluent Society.* New York, 1958.

Garfinkle, Herbert. *When Negroes March.* Glencoe, 1959.

Gladwin, Thomas. *Poverty U.S.A.* Boston, 1967.

Goldman, Eric F. *Rendezvous with Destiny.* New York, 1956.

Goldston, Robert. *The Negro Revolution.* Toronto, 1968.

Gordon, Margaret S. (ed). *Poverty in America.* San Francisco, 1965.

Grant, Joanne. *Black Protest: History, Documents, and Analyses.* Greenwich, 1968.

Gregory, Dick. *Nigger.* New York, 1964.

——. *The Shadow That Scares Me.* New York, 1968.

Grier, William A., and Price M. Cobbs. *Black Rage.* New York, 1968.

Halsell, Grace. *Soul Sister.* Cleveland, 1969.

Harrington, Michael. *The Other America.* New York, 1964.

King, Martin Luther, Jr. *Stride Toward Freedom.* New York, 1958.

——. *Where Do Wo Go From Here?* New York, 1967.

—— *Why We Can't Wait.* New York, 1964.

Leinwand, Gerald. *The Negro in the City.* New York, 1968.

Lester, Julius. *Look Out, Whitey! Black Power's Gonna Get Your Mama.* New York, 1968.

Lincoln, C. Eric. *The Black Muslims in America.* Boston, 1961.

——. *The Negro Pilgrimage in America.* New York, 1967.

——. *Sounds of the Struggle.* New York, 1967.

Lindenmeyer, Otto. *Black History: Lost, Stolen, or Strayed.* New York, 1970.

Lomax, Louis E. *The Negro Revolt.* New York, 1962.

——. *When the Word is Given.* New York, 1963.

Malcolm X, with assistance from Alex Haley. *The Autobiography of Malcolm X.* New York, 1966.

Mannix, Daniel P., and Malcolm Cowley. *Black Cargoes: A History of the Atlantic Slave Trade,* 1518-1865. New York, 1962.

Marine, Gene. *The Black Panthers.* New York, 1969.

Marx, Gary T. *Protest and Prejudice.* New York, 1967.

McWilliams, Carey. *Brothers Under the Skin.* Boston, 1943.

Meier, August, and Elliot M. Rudwick. *From Plantation to Ghetto.* New York, 1966.

Mitchell, J. Paul (ed). *Race Riots in Black and White.* Englewood Cliffs, 1970.

Myrdal, Gunnar. *An American Dilemma.* New York, 1943.

Parsons, Talcott, and Kenneth B. Clark (eds). *The Negro American.* Boston, 1965.

Peck, James. *Freedom Ride.* New York, 1962.

Pettigrew, Thomas F. *A Profile of the Negro American.* Princeton, 1964.

Phillips, U.B. *American Negro Slavery.* New York, 1929.

Quarles, Benjamin. *The Negro in the Civil War.* Boston, 1953.

——. *The Negro in the Making of America.* New York, 1964.

Redding, J. Saunders. *On Being Negro in America.* New York, 1951.

Report of the National Advisory Commission on Civil Disorders. New York, 1968.

Romero, Patricia W. (ed). *In Black America, 1968: The Year of Awakening.* Washington, D.C., 1969.

Ross, Arthur M., and H. Hill (eds). *Employment, Race, and Poverty.* New York, 1967.

St. James, Warren D. *The National Association for the Advancement of Colored People.* New York, 1958.

Schuchter, Arnold. *White Power/Black Freedom: Planning the Future of Urban America.* Boston, 1968.

Schwartz, Barry N., and Robert Disch (eds). *White Racism: Its History, Pathology and Practice.* New York, 1970.

Segal, Ronald. *The Race War.* New York, 1966.

Shoemaker, Don (ed). *With All Deliberate Speed.* New York, 1957.

Silberman, Charles. *Crisis in Black and White.* New York, 1964.

Stampp, Kenneth M. *The Peculiar Institution.* New York, 1956.

Steine, Emma Gelders. *I Have a Dream*. New York, 1965.

Sterling, Dorothy. *Freedom Train: The Story of Harriet Tubman*. Garden City, 1954.

Styron, William. *The Confessions of Nat Turner*. New York, 1967.

Tyack, David. *Nobody Knows: Black Americans in the Twentieth Century*. London, 1969.

Warren, Robert Penn. *Who Speaks for the Negro?* New York, 1965.

Washington, Booker T. *Up from Slavery*. New York, 1901.

Waskow, Arthur. *From Race Riot to Sit-In*. New York, 1966.

Weaver, Robert C. *The Negro Ghetto*. New York, 1948.

Westin, Alan F. (ed). *Freedom Now! The Civil Rights Struggle in America*. New York, 1964.

Woodward, C. Vann. *The Strange Career of Jim Crow*. New York, 1955.

Young, Whitney. *To Be Equal*. New York, 1964.

Articles

Abraham, Henry J. "School Desegregation in the South," *Current History* (August, 1961).

Bennett, Lerone, Jr. "Daisy Bates: First Lady of Little Rock," *Ebony* (September, 1958).

———. "Confrontation on the Campus," *Ebony* (May, 1968).

———. "Stokely Carmichael: Architect of Black Power," *Ebony* (September, 1966).

"Beyond the Riots," *National Review* (August 9, 1966).

"Birth Pangs of Black Capitalism," *Time* (October 18, 1968).

"Black America 1970: Symposium," *Time* (April 6, 1970).

"Black is Beautiful and Belligerent," *Time* (January 24, 1969).

"Black Manifesto," *Time* (May 16, 1969).

"Black Mood on the Campus," *Newsweek* (January 20, 1969).

"Black Moods on the Campus," *Life* (January 31, 1969).

"Black Power Must Be Defined," *Life* (July 22, 1966).

Booker, Simeon. "What the GOP Victory Means for Negroes," *Ebony* (February, 1967).

Carmichael, Stokely. "Power and Racism," *New York Review of Books* (September 22, 1966).

"Civil Rights and the Warren Court," *Ebony* (February, 1970).

"Crisis of Color '66: Survey Findings," *Newsweek* (August 22, 1966).

"Disarray in the Ranks," *Newsweek* (June 17, 1968).

Eckstein, G. "Black Business, Bleak Business," *Nation* (September 15, 1969).

Goodman, G. "Doctor King, One Year After: He Lives, Man!" *Look* (April 15, 1969).

Kilson, M. "Negro Militancy," *Saturday Review* (August 16, 1969).

Marine, Gene, and Adam Hochschild, "Color Black Gloomy," *Ramparts* (December, 1966).

"Mississippi Smiles on Charles Evers," *Life* (May 23, 1969).

Morrison, Allan. " 'New Look' for the Urban League," *Ebony* (November, 1965).

"Negro Cry: Black Power! What Does it Mean?" *U.S. News and World Report* (July 11, 1966).

"Negro Leaders: More Militant Now?" *U.S. News and World Report* (April 22, 1968).

"New Faces, New Voices, New Style," *Newsweek* (June 30, 1969).

"New Racism," *Time* (July 1, 1966).

"Ordeal of the Black Businessman," *Newsweek* (March 4, 1968).

Poinsett, A. "Economics of Liberation," *Ebony* (August, 1969).

"Politics: The White Backlash, 1966," *Newsweek* (October 10, 1966).

Rich, M. "Civil-Rights Progress Out of the Spotlight," *Reporter* (March 7, 1968).

Rudwick, Elliot M. "The Niagara Movement," *Journal of Negro History*, XLII (July, 1957).

Rustin, Bayard. "Myths of the Black Revolt," *Ebony* (August, 1969).

Silberman, Charles E. "The City and the Negro," *Fortune* (March, 1962).

Turner, J. "Student View: Black Students and their Changing Perspective," *Ebony* (August, 1969).

"Violence Justified," *Time* (June 6, 1969).

"What the Negro Has and Has Not Gained: Time Essay," *Time* (October 28, 1966).

"Who Speaks for Negroes Now? A Shift in Leadership," *U.S. News and World Report* (June 23, 1969).

Woodward, C. Vann. "What Happened to the Civil Rights Movement?" *Harper* (January, 1967).

PART TWO. BROWN POWER: THE MEXICAN AMERICANS

Books and Pamphlets

Acuna, Rudy. *A Mexican American Chronicle*. New York, 1971.

Allen, Steve. *The Ground Is Our Table*. Garden City, 1966.

Atwater, James D., and Ramon E. Ruiz. *Out from Under*. Garden City, 1969.

Beck, Warren A. *New Mexico: A History of Four Centuries*. Norman, Okla., 1962.

Bernal, Ignacio. *Mexico Before Cortez: Art, History, and Legend*. Garden City, 1963.

Biran, M.M. *Island in the Crossroads*. Garden City, 1968.

Bishop, C.E. *Farm Labor in the United States*. New York, 1967.

Bolton, Herbert E. *The Spanish Borderlands*. New Haven, 1921.

Burland, C.A. *The Gods of Mexico*. New York, 1968.

Carter, Hodding. *Doomed Road of Empire*. New York, 1971.

Carter, Thomas P. *Mexican Americans in School*. New York (College Entrance Examinations Board), 1970.

Caso, Alfonso. *The Aztecs: People of the Sun*. Norman, Okla., 1958.

Chambers, Clark A. *California Farm Organizations*. Berkeley, 1952.

Clappe, Louise A. *The Shirley Letters from the California Mines*. New York, 1949.

Clendening, Clarence C. *Blood on the Border*. New York, 1969.

Cline, Howard F. *The United States and Mexico*. Cambridge, 1963.

Day, Mark. *Forty Acres: Cesar Chavez and the Farm Workers*. New York, 1971.

Dunne, John Gregory. *Delano: The Story of the California Grape Strike*. New York, 1967.

Forbes, Jack. *Apache, Navaho, and Spaniard*. Norman, Okla., 1960.

Friedland, William H., and Dorothy Nelkin. *Migrant: Agricultural Workers in America's Northwest*. New York, 1971.

Galarza, Ernesto. *Merchants of Labor: The Mexican Bracero Story, 1942-1960*. Santa Barbara, 1964.

———, Herman Gallegos, and Julian Samora. *Mexican-Americans in the Southwest*. Santa Barbara, 1969.

Gamio, Manuel. *Mexican Immigration to the United States*. Chicago, 1930.

Gardner, Richard. *Grito*. Indianapolis, 1970.

Grebler, Leo, Joan W. Moore, and Ralph C. Guzman. *The Mexican-American People*. New York, 1970.

Heller, Celia S. *Mexican American Youth*. New York, 1966.

Hollon, William E. *The Southwest: Old and New*. New York, 1961.

Horgan, Paul. *Conquistadores in North American History*. New York, 1963.

Lamb, Ruth S. *Mexican Americans: Sons of the Southwest*. Claremont, Calif., 1970.

La Raza Unida Party in Texas. Speeches by Mario Compean and José Angel Gutierrez. Introduction by Antonio Camezo. A Merit Pamphlet from Pathfinder Press. New York, 1970.

Leon- Portilla, Miguel. *The Broken Spears*. Boston, 1962.

Ludwig, Ed, and James Santibanez (eds). *The Chicanos: Mexican American Voices*. Baltimore, 1971.

Madson, William. *The Mexican Americans of South Texas*. New York, 1964.

Matthiessen, Peter. *Sal Si Puedes: Cesar Chavez and the New American Revolution*. New York, 1969.

McWilliams, Carey. *The Mexicans in America*. New York, 1969.

———. *North from Mexico*. New York, 1968.

Meier, Matt S., and Feliciano Rivera. *The Chicanos: A History of the Mexican Americans*. New York, 1972.

Meinig, Donald W. *Southwest: Three Peoples in Geographical Change, 1600-1970*. New York, 1971.

Moore, Joan W., and Alfredo Cuellar. *Mexican Americans*. Englewood Cliffs, 1970.

Moore, Truman E. *The Slaves We Rent*. New York, 1965.

Moquin, Wayne (ed). *A Documentary History of the Mexican American*. New York, 1971.

forting)

Morin, Raul. *Among the Valiant*. Los Angeles, 1963.

Nabokov, Peter. *Tijerina and the Courthouse Raid*. Albuquerque, 1969.

Nava, Julian. *Mexican Americans: Past, Present and Future*. Cincinnati, 1969.

Paz, Octavio. *The Labyrinth of Solitude*. Translated by Lysander Kemp. New York, 1961.

Peterson, Frederick A. *Ancient Mexico*. New York, 1959.

Pitt, Leonard. *The Decline of the Californios: A Social History of the Spanish-Speaking Californians, 1846-1890*. Berkeley, 1966.

Rappaport, Armin. *The War with Mexico: Why Did It Happen?* New York, 1964.

Rendon, Armando B. *Chicano Manifesto*. New York, 1971.

Rivera, Feliciano. *A Mexican American Source Book*. Menlo Park, Calif., 1970.

Rubel, Arthur J. *Across the Tracks: Mexican-Americans in a Texas City*. Austin, 1966.

Samora, Julian (ed). *La Raza: Forgotten Americans*. Notre Dame, 1966.

Sanchez, David (Prime Minister, Brown Berets). *Chicano Power Explained*. Undated Pamphlet supplied by Brown Berets c/o *La Raza*, P.O. Box 31004, Los Angeles, California 90031.

Sanchez, George I. *Forgotten People: A Study of New Mexicans*. Albuquerque, 1940.

Servins, Manuel. *The Mexican Americans: An Awakening Minority*. Beverly Hills, Calif., 1970.

Shotwell, Louisa R. *The Harvesters: The Story of the Migrant People*. Garden City, 1961.

Simmen, Edward (ed). *The Chicano: From Caricature to Self-Portrait*. New York, 1971.

Steiner, Stan. *La Raza: The Mexican Americans*. New York, 1969.

Tebhel, J., and Ramon E. Ruiz. *South by Southwest*. Garden City, 1969.

Wolf, Eric. *Sons of the Shaking Earth*. Chicago, 1959.

Articles and Reports

"Another Civil Rights Headache—Plight of the Mexican-Americans," *U.S. News and World Report* (June 6, 1966).

Blauner, R. "Chicano Sensibility," *Trans-Action* (February, 1971).

Bongartz, Roy. "La Raza in Revolt," *Nation* (June 1, 1970).

"Changing Time," *Nation* (November 3, 1969).

"Chicanos Campaign for a Better Deal," *Business Week* (May 29, 1971).

"Chicanos Riot," *Time* (September 7, 1970).

Coles, Robert, and Harry Huge. "Thorns on the Yellow Rose of Texas," *New Republic* (April 19, 1969).

Coyne, John R., Jr. "Grapes of Wrath," *National Review* (July 1, 1969).

Crusade for Justice, 1567 Downing, Denver, Colorado. Unpublished materials supplied, including a biographical sketch of Rodolfo Gonzales; an outline of "The Spiritual Plan of Aztlan"; a history of the Crusade for Justice; and assorted speeches by R. Gonzales.

Dunne, John Gregory. "To Die Standing: Cesar Chavez and the Chicanos," *Atlantic* (June, 1971).

Gomez, David F. "Chicanos Besieged: the Bloody Fiesta," *Nation* (March 15, 1971).

———. "Killing of Ruben Salazar: Nothing Has Really Changed in the Barrio," *The Christian Century* (January 13, 1971).

Hearing Before the United States Commission on Civil Rights Held at Our Lady of the Lake College, San Antonio, Texas, December 9-14, 1968. U.S. Government Printing Office, Washington, D.C.

Heller, Celia S. "Chicano Is Beautiful," *Commonweal* (January 23, 1970).

Justin, Neal. "Culture, Conflict, and Mexican-American Achievement," *School and Society* (January, 1970).

"La Raza: the Race for Equality," *Senior Scholastic* (January 10, 1972).

"Little Strike that Grew to *La Causa*," *Time* (July 4, 1969).

Lopez, Enrique Hank. "Overkill at the Silver Dollar," *Nation* (October 19, 1970).

Macias, Ysidro Ramon. "Chicano Movement," *Wilson Library Bulletin* (March, 1970).

McNamara, Patrick H. "Rumbles Along the Rio," *Commonweal* (March 14, 1969).

"Mexican-Americans: the Nation's Best-kept Secret?" *Senior Scholastic* (April 18, 1969).

Nabokov, Peter. "La Raza, the Land and the Hippies," *Nation* (April 20, 1970).

Ortego, P.D. "Schools for Mexican-Americans: Between Two Cultures," *Saturday Review* (April 17, 1971).

"Out of History into the Barrios," *Business Week* (May 29, 1971).

Phillips, N.D. "Chicano Workers, Rio Grande Farmers Agree to Meet," *The Christian Century* (January 20, 1971).

Post, D. "Mexican-Americans and La Raza," *The Christian Century* (March 5, 1969).

Rees, L., and P. Montague. "Ford and La Raza: They Stole Our Land and Gave Us Powdered Milk," *Ramparts* (September, 1970).

Rechy, John. "No Mañanas for Today's Chicanos," *Saturday Review* (March 14, 1970).

"Schools Fail Chicanos," *America* (September 12, 1970).

Steiner, Stan. "Chicano Power," *New Republic* (June 20, 1970).

"Tio Taco is Dead," *Newsweek* (June 29, 1970).

U. S. Bureau of the Census. *Current Population Reports,* Series P-20, No. 213, "Persons of Spanish Origin in the United States: November 1969." U.S. Government Printing Office, Washington, D.C., 1971.

Newspapers Consulted

Chicano Student Movement, P.O. Box 31322, Los Angeles, Calif. 90031.

El Gallo, 1265 Cherokee St., Denver, Colorado 80204.

El Grito Del Norte, Rt. 2, Box 5, Espanola, N.M. 87532.

Inside Eastside, P.O. Box 63273, Los Angeles, Calif. 90063.

Lado, 1306 N. Western Ave., Chicago, Ill. 60622.
El Malcriado, P.O. Box 130, Delano, Calif. 93215.
La Raza, P.O. Box 31004, Los Angeles, Calif. 90031.

PART THREE. RED POWER: THE AMERICAN INDIAN

Books
Bakeless, John. *Eyes of Discovery.* New York, 1961.
Baldwin, Gordon C. *America's Buried Past.* New York, 1962.
Barret, S.M. (ed). *Geronimo: His Own Story.* New York, 1970.
Benedict, Ruth. *Patterns of Culture.* Boston, 1934.
Boas, Franz. *Race, Language and Culture.* New York, 1949.
Brennan, Louis A. *No Stone Unturned.* New York, 1959.
Brown, Dee. *Bury My Heart at Wounded Knee: An Indian History of the American West.* New York, 1970.
——. *Showdown at Little Bighorn.* New York, 1964.
Cheshire, Giff. *Thunder on the Mountain.* New York, 1960.
Chronicles of American Indian Protest. Compiled and edited by the Council on Interracial Books for Children. Greenwich, 1971.
Collier, John. *Indians of the Americas.* New York, 1947.
Deloria, Vine, Jr. *Custer Died for Your Sins: An Indian Manifesto.* New York, 1969.
—— (ed). *Of Utmost Good Faith.* New York, 1971.
——. *We Talk, You Listen.* New York, 1970.
Drucker, Philip. *Indians of the Northwest Coast.* New York, 1955.
Fey, Harold E., and D'Arcy McNickle. *Indians and Other Americans.* New York, 1959.
Gladwin, Harold S. *Men Out of Asia.* New York, 1947.
Gridley, Marion E. (ed). *Indians of Today.* Third Edition. Chicago, 1960.
Griffin, James B. (ed). *Archaeology of Eastern United States.* Chicago, 1952.
Hoebel, E. Adamson. *Anthropology: The Study of Man.* New York, 1949.
Jennings, Jesse D. *Prehistory of North America.* New York, 1968.
Josephy, Alvin M., Jr. *The Indian Heritage of America.* New York, 1968.
—— (ed). *Red Power: The American Indians' Fight for Freedom.* New York, 1971.
Kroeber, Theodora. *Ishi in Two Worlds.* Berkeley, 1961.
La Farge, Oliver. *A Pictorial History of the American Indian.* New York, 1956.
Lowie, Robert H. *Indians of the Plains.* New York, 1954.
MacLeod, William C. *The American Indian Frontier.* New York, 1928.
Marriott, Alice. *The First Comers.* New York, 1960.
——, and Carol K. Rachlin. *American Epic: The Story of the American Indians.* New York, 1969.
Martin, Paul S., and others. *Indians Before Columbus.* Chicago, 1947.
McNickle, D'Arcy. *The Indian Tribes of the United States.* New York, 1962.

Memoirs of Chief Red Fox. Introduction by Cash Asher. Greenwich, 1971.

Neihardt, John G. *Black Elk Speaks.* New York, 1932.

Radin, Paul. *The Story of the American Indian.* New York, 1957.

Reno, Philip. *Taos Pueblo.* Chicago, 1963.

Shorris, Earl. *The Death of the Great Spirit: An Elegy for the American Indian.* New York, 1971.

Silverberg, Robert. *Home of the Red Man: Indian North America Before Columbus.* New York, 1963.

Spencer, Robert F., Jesse D. Jennings, and others. *The Native Americans.* New York, 1965.

Spicer, Edward H. *A Short History of the Indians of the United States.* New York, 1969.

Steiner, Stan. *The New Indians.* New York, 1968.

Tebbel, John. *The Compact History of the Indian Wars.* New York, 1966.

Underhill, Ruth M. *Red Man's America.* Chicago, 1953.

Van Every, Dale. *Disinherited.* New York, 1966.

Waters, Frank. *The Book of the Hopi.* New York, 1963.

Wauchope, Robert. *Lost Tribes and Sunken Continents.* Chicago, 1962.

Wilson, Edmund. *Apologies to the Iroquois.* New York, 1959.

Wissler, Clark. *The American Indians.* New York, 1950.

———. *Indians of the United States.* Garden City, 1940.

———. *Red Man Reservations.* New York, 1938.

Articles and Reports

"Americans for Indian Opportunity." An undated report and summary issued by the A.I.O., 1820 Jefferson Place, N.W., Washington, D.C. 20036. Received, Spring, 1972.

"American Indians Come Nearer the Mainstream," *Business Week* (June 7, 1969).

"American Indians: the Right to be Themselves," *Senior Scholastic* (October 13, 1969).

"Angry American Indian—Starting Down the Protest Trail," *Time* (February 9, 1970).

"Anomy at Alcatraz," *Time* (April 12, 1971).

Bauman, J.F. "Forgotten Americans: the Migrant and the Indian Poor," *Current History* (June, 1973).

"Behind the Indian Uprising: What they Have and Want," *U.S. News & World Report* (November 20, 1972).

Bennett, Lerone, Jr. "Red and Black: the Indians and the Africans," *Ebony* (December, 1970).

Bongartz, Roy. "The New Indian," *Esquire* (August, 1970).

Boyer, S. "Blazing a New Trail," *Saturday Review* (January 16, 1971).

Boyle, Kay. "A Day on Alcatraz with the Indians," *New Republic* (January 17, 1970).

Bureau of Indian Affairs. *Answers to your Questions about American Indians.* U.S. Government Printing Office, Washington, D.C. 20402. April, 1970.

Bureau of Indian Affairs. *Federal Indian Policies,* "A Summary of Major Developments from the Pre-Revolutionary Period through the 1960's." U.S. Government Printing Office, Washington, D.C. 20402. Undated.

Collier, Peter. "American Thing: White Society is Breaking Down Around Us. . . ." Interview with Vine Deloria, Jr., *Mademoiselle* (April, 1971).

———. "Red Man's Burden," *Ramparts* (February, 1970).

———. "Salmon Fishing in America: the Indians Vs. the State of Washington," *Ramparts* (April, 1971).

"Death at Wounded Knee," *Time* (May 7, 1973).

Degler, C.N. "Indians and Other Americans," *Commentary* (November, 1972).

Deloria, Vine, Jr. "Theological Dimension of the Indian Protest Movement," *The Christian Century* (September 19, 1973).

———. "This Country was a Lot Better Off When the Indians were Running It," *New York Times Magazine* (March 8, 1970).

———. "War Between the Redskins and the Feds," *New York Times Magazine* (December 7, 1969).

"Drums Along the Potomac," *Newsweek* (November 20, 1972).

Erickson, D.A. "Failure in Navajo Schooling," *Parents' Magazine* (September, 1970).

Fey, Harold E. "America's Most Oppressed Minority," *The Christian Century* (January 20, 1971).

Fuchs, E. "Time to Redeem an Old Promise," *Saturday Review* (January 24, 1970).

Hedgepeth, William. "Alcatraz: the Indian Uprising that Worked," *Look* (June 2, 1970).

"Indian in the City," *Newsweek* (June 14, 1971).

"Indians: the Great Spirit," *Newsweek* (May 14, 1973).

"Industry Invades the Reservation," *Business Week* (April 4, 1970).

Josephy, Alvin M. "Custer Myth," *Life* (July 2, 1971).

Kanton, Seth. "Indian Wool Makes the Grade," *Nation's Business* (January, 1972).

Kennedy, Edward M. "Let the Indians Run Indian Policy," *Look* (June 2, 1970).

"Land They Loved and Lost: the Menominee Indian Story," *Senior Scholastic* (November 13, 1972).

"Managing Cash the Tribal Way: Jicarilla Apache Tribe," *Business Week* (December 26, 1970).

Mangel, Charles. "Sometimes We Feel We're Already Dead: Arizona's Ruined Cocopah," *Look* (June 2, 1970).

Maxey, David R. "Bureau of Indian Affairs: America's Colonial Service," *Look* (June 2, 1970).

Meyer, E.I. "Bury My Heart on the Potomac," *Ramparts* (January, 1973).

Momaday, N. Scott. "Visions Beyond Time and Place," *Life* (July 2, 1971).

Morris, T. "La Donna Harris: A Woman Who Gives a Damn," *Redbook* (February, 1970).

Nabokov, Peter. "Our Most Silent Minority," *Nation* (January 26, 1970).

"Navajos Trade Hogans for Air Conditioning: Shiprock Housing Project," *Business Week* (October 23, 1971).

"New Deal Coming for American Indians?" *U.S. News & World Report* (September 14, 1970).

Oakes, R. "Alcatraz is not an Island," *Ramparts* (December, 1972).

Schonbach, Samuel. "What the Red Man Needs," *Catholic World* (November, 1971).

Tunley R. "Smooth Path at Rough Rock," *American Education* (March, 1971).

Witten, Edward. "Are you Listening, D.H. Lawrence?" *New Republic* (October 18, 1969).

*Interviews**

Dennis Banks, National Field Director of the American Indian Movement. Grand Rapids, Michigan. October, 1973.

George Bennet, director of the Indian Affairs Commission for Michigan. Lansing, Michigan. August, 1973.

Eddie Benton, one of the founders of the American Indian Movement and past director of AIM-St. Paul. Telephone Interview. October, 1973.

Russell Means, National Field Director for the American Indian Movement. Detroit, Michigan. December, 1973.

Ramon Roubideaux, chief legal counsellor for the American Indian Movement. Grand Rapids, Michigan. October, 1973.

Mel Thom, one of the founders and first president of the National Indian Youth Council. Telephone Interview. October, 1973.

Gerald Wilkinson, executive director of the National Indian Youth Council. Telephone Interview. October, 1973.

* For the sake of space I have listed only nationally known figures.